FRANCO

The Succulent

outskirts
press

Dedication

This book is dedicated to the one person who reads it and finds something within its pages that brings more love, joy, peace, and happiness into their life.

I love you.
Keep fighting forward!

—Larry

#JustSaveOne

Acknowledgments

I wish to thank Save A Warrior and all of the generous people who donate to support their mission. Without it, this book would not exist, because I would not be around to write it.

I consider it a miracle that Save A Warrior and I crossed paths when we did, and for the experience itself.

I am most thankful for my wife, Sue, who journeyed with me into and out of Complex PTS (thirty-three years thus far), lovingly stayed by my side, and afterward went through the program herself.

I thank those who came back for me and showed me the path out of the Complex PTS insanity I was in.

I'm thankful for the mentors and fellow travelers who stuck with me as I crawled my way from insanity to reality. Recovery is not easy work, and I am appreciative of all that do the work on themselves.

I wish to thank all of the great people I've met in the rooms of recovery who freely share their life-saving wisdom with anyone who asks, with no strings attached.

I follow the other warriors on this path before me, as long as they have something that I want. Sanity, sobriety, confidence, peace, and joy.

If they have it, and I want it, I gotta do what you do in order to get it.

Once I have it, if I want to keep it, I have to give it away.

In that manner, we all walk together toward the same goal.

I also wish to thank Megan Cox, who painted the artistic backdrop on the covers.

—Larry

Foreword

I've never written a forward before and certainly never have been asked to do so until Larry honored me with that request just a few days before he completed this book. Larry and I both work/serve at Save A Warrior and have dedicated our lives to helping others recover from Complex PTS and Suicidal Ideation. There's something you gotta get about Larry. He's a certifiable badass! Maybe some of you reading this will have the joy of meeting him one day, or if you are ready to be done suffering, and apply to Save A Warrior, perhaps he will be the one doing your rostering call. Now, Larry being the badass that he is, a US Army veteran, and a retired law enforcement officer, who visually, to one who doesn't know Larry, might appear as one scary dude. But once he starts speaking, a fountain of wisdom and, oftentimes humor, starts pouring from his heart, in a language that touches the very core of each person he interacts with. Larry is a very humble man who prefers to be a "nobody" and just spread joy and love wherever he goes. So, convincing him to stop deleting all the essays and books he wrote and compile them into a book he would actually publish was quite a task!

You see, people like Larry, myself, and many if not most in the Warrior Class (veterans and first responders), have a lot of significance around our identities and affiliations we've built with our units and professions. There was a day when if you asked me who I was, I'd say I was a veteran, infantryman, or some other profession-based identity. My significance in my professional identity was a way of covering up that I didn't really know who I was, or that I had a lot of shame around who I believed I was. For me, it was a combo platter of both. I hated myself. I truly believed I was the worst human being on the planet. I believed that I was a mistake and that my existence was invalid, so I had to create false identities, personalities, and ways of being to get my needs met. I also developed a compulsive need to control every possible outcome, in every situation I was in, to have a sense of peace and security. What I was blind to was each attempt at controlling the future was digging me deeper into a pit of despair.

The only way to predict the future is by looking at the past, and I was spending so much of my life riddled with anxiety, hypervigilance, stress, fear, and sadness, trying to control every aspect of the future, so that the past would not repeat itself, thinking that the next move on the game board would be the thing that would fix everything. I was actually projecting my past onto the future and living in a future dictated by my past. All the while, I was never present in the moment, which is the only place peace and serenity can occur. I was so wrapped up in my significance that I never realized I was abandoning myself the whole time.

I had Complex PTS, which began in childhood from not having a fully formed sense of self, left to do my best to survive in a dysfunctional family of poverty, abuse, violence, and addiction. I had to develop survival traits that became my default setting in how I showed up in life, to those around me, and by the time I showed up to Save A Warrior at thirty-six years old, I didn't know that I didn't know I had been living my entire life in a vicious circle (we talk funny here). I was repeating the same behaviors, over and over, knowing exactly how it would turn out, and doing it anyway. I had previously been certain that the problems in my life were from what happened to me in Iraq, when I was deployed there from 2003 to 2004. My mental health professionals supported my beliefs. It wasn't until I went to Save A Warrior that I realized that it wasn't so much PTSD that I had been suffering from; rather, it was formative trauma from my childhood, collapsed with adulthood moral injury. I felt awake and aware for the first time, and these were people who were speaking a language that sounded funny, but at the same time, made perfect sense. These were wounded healers, who had recovered from the same things I had been suffering from, and they were coming back for ME of all people. Parts of me didn't feel worthy or deserving, but I wanted what they had, so I did what they did. I was honest, open, and willing. I was vulnerable and coachable. I was ready to be done suffering.

A big discovery for me, and for many who come to Save A Warrior, is that I must let go of my significance and just be an ordinary human being, having a human being experience. My suffering is not that special, I am not that special, and I MUST take responsibility for my life. I was blaming all of my life's problems on others, never realizing that the only one who was responsible was me. That doesn't mean that others didn't have a part to play in what happened to me, but rather than living in resentments and stirring up drama around those people, places, and things, I can be complete with it and let it be. I own my side of the street, take responsibility for it, and move forward with my life. What other people have done, or have not done, really doesn't matter, as it's in the past, and the past can't be changed. All that matters is what I am doing to continue to heal myself, right here, right now. A key piece of that is working with others and leading them through the same work that I was led through. So today, I lead others through this work. I work with others in 12-step rooms ending in "Anonymous," I fellow travel with men who are also on this path with me, and each time I share my story with others and lead them to the solution, or at least what the solution could look like, I get back what I gave ten-fold (spiritually speaking). I don't get mine until you get yours.

If you are a veteran who is ready to be done suffering, I encourage you to read this book, go to saveawarrior.org and thoroughly read through the website, and submit an application. Let's have a conversation and see if we are a good fit for each other. Save A Warrior saved my life, and for that, I am eternally grateful.

Thank you for listening to me, and I hope you enjoy reading Larry's book as much as I did. This is just a snapshot of some of the things we talk about regularly at Save A Warrior, and hear this the right way: none of us has a patent on healing. All the information is out there, in thousands of books, and in hundreds and hundreds of self-help programs. You just have to "look." Save A Warrior has distilled the best parts of it into their program, and the novel way in which it is presented, along with the honest conversations had, can and will transform your life, if you are willing to stand in the possibility that maybe, just maybe, what these people are talking about might be true.

Joe Robb
Save A Warrior Cohort 0109

Table of Contents

Preface

Me: "Make sure it's the book you want."

Franco: "What's that you say?"

Me: "Oh. It's something my mentor told me the other day. He told me, 'Larry, write a book, but make sure it's the book you want.' Hmm…"

Franco: "So, what's the problem?"

Me: "Well, I don't know how to write a book, I guess, is the big problem. There are many problems, but that would probably be the biggest one, not knowing how to write one."

Franco: "I see. And has not knowing what you are doing ever slowed you?"

Me: "That's a good point. No, it has not. Thank you."

Franco: "That's what I'm here for. That, and beautifying your office."

Me: "He also said, 'Don't make it all crazy. Just keep it simple.'"

Franco: "Is that when you told him you were talking to a houseplant through the whole thing as your big idea?"

Me: "Nah, I didn't mention that part. I figured it would be just one of those things that I ask forgiveness for afterward instead of permission."

Franco: "You seem to have many of those moments, almost like it's a life code."

Me: "I like the word 'mischievous.' I can be mischievous. When I struggle to accomplish something, what helps is if I hold myself accountable to others. In this case, I promised I would have a book done by June 10th.

"I have a history of disappointing and breaking my word to myself throughout life. All humans do. When I give my word that I will do something or stop doing something to another person, I am more likely to accomplish that goal because now my integrity is on the line.

"I have also discovered that I am not terminally unique about anything. There is a verse in the book of Ecclesiastes that states:

'What has been done will be done again; there is nothing new under the sun.'"

Franco: "What, is thing going to be a religious book?"

Me: "Not really. I don't shun any religion, however. I use that as a reference to the point that the fact that none of us is terminally unique has been spoken about for thousands of years.

"I have found that when I judge something or someone to be 'wrong,' the only one I am punishing is myself. Judging others to be wrong prevents me from gaining access to their wisdom, and there is a lot of wisdom to be found in various religions. Christianity, Buddhism, Islam, Hinduism, etc. I study all of them. Christianity is the one I am most familiar with, thus the first one I referenced. Judging others to be wrong is what I used to do back when my life didn't work, and I ended up going through a suicide prevention program called Save A Warrior.

"Fear of judgment being cast upon me kept me from living a fully expressed life, spiritually isolating myself from meaningful connections and relationships with anyone else.

I didn't even know I was doing that until someone else pointed it out to me.

"Fear of shame and judgment all my life is what caused me to travel down a particular pathway in life in which suicide eventually seemed like a very logical and honorable thing to do.

"So this book is not going to be religious. However, it will be spiritual, and it will be about Save A Warrior. I will mostly be speaking from a spiritual point of view. Depression, anxiety, and suicidal ideation are spiritual concerns, which is why the material solutions such as anti-anxiety/anti-depressants often only work for a limited time. They work for a while, but like all drugs, the human body eventually builds a tolerance to them, and after a while, they quit working. Then there's often a steep drop-off when they do."

Franco: "That's why they call Save A Warrior 'The Last House on the Block'?"

Me: "Absolutely. Veterans and first responders struggling with Complex PTS usually come to Save A Warrior after they've exhausted all other means to end their suffering, sometimes after multiple suicide attempts. They've tried everything else out there and come here with the desperation of a drowning person. That's actually perfect because that usually means that they're open to some new ideas.

"I remind the people that I roster into the program that my way of thinking and managing my life has led me to Save A Warrior, which is a Complex PTS, suicidal ideation detox facility.

So maybe I'm open to some new ideas and a new way of looking at life.

"We need that sort of openness and willingness because we're gonna talk about some stuff in a way other organizations cannot. There's a novelty to it. We talk funny."

Franco: "What's that mean?"

Me: "Well, first of all, there's no transaction to get into here. The person coming in never receives a bill of any sort. I tell folks, 'You won't get a bill, a pill, or a disorder diagnosis. We don't want anything from you. We only want for you.' And furthermore, 'You don't have anything that I want.'

"I reiterate that your way of playing the game of life based upon your wisdom has led you here, a suicide prevention program. No one comes here because they've recently won the lottery or anything. They come here because their lives are filled with suffering, and typically they don't even know why. They think they do. Many of them have survived incredibly traumatic experiences in the veteran/first responder worlds, and they point to those experiences as the reasons why they're struggling in life.

"The real reasons they're struggling have nothing to do with those particular experiences, and they don't know that. That means we're not going to argue or entertain conversations filled with arguments or entertain questions filled with 'Yeah but, how about, what ifs.' We're not here to get into any philosophical debates with anyone.

"I'll tell them, 'If you're pleased with how your life is panning out under your management, by all means, kick that can on down the road and keep doing things your way. Come back when you're more open.' They have to have that sort of mindset, or they will miss out on the experience."

Franco: "So that's what you do, you get people into the program?"

Me: "I roster people into the program. I'm part of a rostering team. An individual who meets the qualifications (veteran/first responder) submits an application to get into the program, then another member of the team or I have a conversation with them to determine whether or not Save A Warrior is going to be a good fit for them."

Franco: "What are you looking for in those conversations?"

Me: "I don't want to give away any part of the game, but I can assure you, it's not going to go your way. Someone is not going to get a seat in the program simply because they are a veteran or first responder. Some come with the mentality that they deserve a seat simply due to their status as a veteran or first responder, and that is not the case.

"The pathway we have found out of Complex PTS is one of unwavering honesty. That means we're going to stick to the truth, even if we don't like what the truth has to say, we stick to the truth anyway because it's the truth.

"Vulnerability is a key component to everything, so in the rostering conversation, I am going to ask some questions people are typically hesitant to answer. Sometimes the person will evade the question by telling a war story, which is a very common conversational tactic to avoid vulnerability, and I will direct them back to the original question. That demonstrates the third component required for transformation."

Franco: "Coachability."

Me: "Spot on, a willingness to try things our way. Some of the war stories are very horrific. I will listen to them for a bit, and then directly ask them if they're coachable. If they say yes, I repeat the question, maybe more slowly the second time. Honest questions deserve honest answers.

"Suppose they continue to resist answering the question. In that case, they will probably not get much out of the Save A Warrior experience and possibly ruin the experience for others, so I don't roster them.

"I have empathy for them, but this is not the VA or a counseling session that one has paid for. We are not going to avoid the truth here.

"Mind you, I was probably one of the biggest assholes to ever come through the program. I fought their wisdom the whole time I was there. I resisted it quite a bit and almost wrecked the entire cohort experience for the others who were there with me."

Franco: "But you eventually got it."

Me: "I did, it was a miracle! But the founder said I made him work too hard for it. So my job in the rostering call is to make sure people like me who are coming to argue come back when they're more willing.

"Consider it more of an initiation into our community. To be initiated into any organization, you have to want what I have. You don't have anything I want. I'm not coming to you. You're coming to me. In order to get initiated into our community, you have to do things our way, which is going to be wildly different than the way we are accustomed to. That's what makes us unique as an organization. To have a seat at the table in Save A Warrior, one has to be honest, open, and willing. We're looking for vulnerability and authenticity, or at least the ingredients for it.

"Getting through the conversation that will transform one's life at SAW requires courage. Courage is different than bravery. Bravery is running toward bullets or running into a burning building. Courage is standing in the truth and fearlessly owning responsibility for one's own decisions and actions in life and not passing the buck or blaming others.

"Now, if one can combine the two, bravery and courage, that typically creates an incredibly powerful person who can reclaim their own life."

Franco: "So that's what this book is about then?"

Me: "Not really."

Franco: "What? What is this book about?"

Me: "Nothing in particular. It's just a book written by a person who was once self-diagnosed as 'bat-shit crazy' and who had a spiritual awakening of the educational variety as a result of going through Save A Warrior's program.

"The entire way I saw life and the universe shifted dramatically after that. I immediately started seeking wisdom and applying the wisdom I found to my life, and my view of life improved. I went from being suicidally depressed to thoroughly enjoying my life experience. I often write about these things on social media because I want others to be aware of some things that have improved my life in case they have the same experience."

Franco: "We are all beggars, trying to show other beggars where to find bread."

Me: "And none of us being terminally unique, if I find something in life that makes my life experience better, I am compelled to share it with others. Maybe someone out there will relate to it, and their perspective on life will improve.

"That being said, I only speak the truth. However, no one should take this book as the absolute truth. Remember, I was once self-diagnosed as 'bat-shit crazy,' and there would be a line out the door of people who know me or have worked alongside of me that will tell you, 'That's actually a very accurate assessment.'"

Franco: "Wait, you say you only speak the truth, but no one should take what you say in this book as the truth? Do I understand that correctly? That doesn't make sense."

Me: "Back up to the part in which I mentioned I was 'bat-shit crazy' and pause on that. Soak it in for a bit. I'm talking to you, and you are a houseplant."

Franco: "How dare you! I am a succulent, I'll have you know!"

Me: "Sounds like someone is stuck on their own significance a bit. It's been my experience in life that when I am certain that I have found the absolute truth about something in life, God always chuckles and changes things up for me. Thinking one knows the absolute truth, in general, creates what I like to describe as 'assholes.' Those are people who are certain that their way of doing things or knowing things is the only way to view a particular issue. Those people tend to be very opinionated, unopen, and unwilling to consider new information or perspectives."

Franco: "Assholes."

Me: "Right. I was a huge asshole when I came to Save A Warrior. Parts of me are still an asshole, and I still have my opinions on various subjects. I will try to keep my opinions to myself. You know what they say about opinions and assholes?"

Franco: "Everybody has one, and they all stink."

Me: "Right. So this is just a book of things that I've noticed in life, part of my experience, and have decided to share in case it helps out anyone else.

"I will also try to avoid war stories in this book. I might mention some of my life experiences in as much as how 'what happened' caused me to have a particular perspective in life and how that perspective later changed.

"For me, the telling of war stories for the sake of telling war stories serves no purpose other than to inflate the storyteller's ego. Sometimes I ask people to observe. 'Notice in the war stories we tell that we only tell the ones that make us the victim or hero. We never tell the ones in which we are the suspect. Isn't that curious?'

"There might be a chapter or two about 'how it was, what happened, and how I see things now.' Typically the telling of war stories causes a person to dwell on the past."

Franco: "Dwelling in the past is the major cause of depression."

Me: "Unless one is honestly and purposely seeking gratitude, as I've come to find out."

Franco: "Dope."

Me: "Quit trying to sound cool, Franco. You're a houseplant."

Franco: "A succulent! I am a succulent."

Me: "Your ego is not your amigo, my chill green friend."

Franco: "I'm chill, my brother from a human mother. So, I'm still trying to sort this. This is a book in which you, a person who only speaks the truth, is not professing to tell the truth."

Me: "Right, these are just some of my observations. Some of these I post on social media and am told have helped others in their struggles. Or they're just things that I am relating to you, my succulent."

Franco: "Thank you, my human."

Integrity

Me: "Perhaps the most powerful line written in the book of Alcoholics Anonymous is the second line of chapter 5: 'How it works' and states, 'Those who do not recover are people… who are constitutionally incapable of being honest with themselves.'

"I've omitted the middle part of the sentence as it applies to the AA program, but I think the wisdom of the sentence applies to a whole lot more than just the AA program. It also applies to Complex PTS, which is what I struggled with."

Franco: "You don't still struggle with it?"

Me: "Maybe. I think all humans do to some degree. All humans have struggles in life. That's what life is, a series of 'problems' that I choose to resolve, accept, or ignore. I'm faced with many of the same challenges all others deal with, the difference being I took the wisdom of that statement and examined myself pretty thoroughly, with integrity in my search.

"When I noticed that I was, in fact, struggling with some aspect of my life, instead of denying that I was struggling (common human behavior), I admitted my shortcomings, took responsibility for them, and did things to correct those errors.

"I have essentially rearranged parts of my life to overcome those parts that I struggled with. I created a daily routine, certain things I do each day at the same time, such as meditation. Meditation allows me to control the focus of my mind easier so I can catch myself early on when a struggle is beginning.

"Controlling the focus of one's mind is crucial to being able to enjoy life. Everything I experience in life, I internally label the experience as 'good' or 'bad.' The label I attach to the thing I am experiencing is entirely dependent upon my perspective.

"There are things in the world I can control and change, and there are things I cannot control and change. Wisdom is knowing the difference."

Franco: "Hey, that's the Serenity Prayer!"

Me: "Indeed. That is a very powerful, short little prayer:

'God grant me the serenity to accept the things I cannot change,
The courage to change the things I can,
And the wisdom to know the difference.'

"If I'm spending my time trying to manipulate people and things that are beyond my power to change, my life will be filled with feelings of frustration and uselessness.

"I cannot control other people, nor can I control what they think of me. That is something only God has influence over. When I try to do that, I am a god with no power."

Franco: "And nothing is more frustrated and angry than a god with no power."

Me: "You're on fire this morning."

Franco: "I am? Where? Put it out! Put it out!"

Me: "That's just an expression, Franco. You're not actually on fire; I just meant you are on a winning streak."

Franco: "Please be careful with your words!"

Me: "See? There you go again!

"Getting back to the original topic, when I first read the sentence, 'Those who do not recover are people...who are constitutionally incapable of being honest with themselves,' I had to look inward to examine myself. I asked myself, 'Can I be honest with myself?' and looked inward for the answer.

"I decided, yes, I can be. It doesn't matter if I am lying to everyone else out there in the world. As long as I vowed never to lie to myself, I now have something I didn't have when I was suicidal. I suddenly had hope.

"I took the sentence to be a piece of wisdom that didn't just apply to people who identified themselves as alcoholics. The wisdom applied to anyone who was struggling with life in any way.

"To resolve a problem, I first have to admit to myself that there is, in fact, a problem. If I don't admit that there's a problem in my life, I'll attempt to fix it. Not fixing a problem causes it to get worse, and worse, which leads to myself wanting to numb my life experience in some fashion, in this case, with alcohol. But it doesn't have to be alcohol. There are a thousand ways to numb and avoid acceptance of one's present circumstances in life.

"To even begin this journey of unfucking my life, I have to determine if I have integrity. Does my word hold any value, yes or no? If the answer is no, and I decide that my word has no value, then I'm screwed. If the answer is yes, my word does indeed have value, then I can begin addressing and fixing some of the things that I admit to myself are a problem.

"Even if I have examined myself and decided that my word has no value, not even to myself, there's still hope for me. I can decide that starting now, right now, I will never lie to myself and begin to build integrity within myself. It's a simple decision, really. That decision occurs starting right now."

Franco: "The only moment in time that truly exists."

Me: "Don't distract me and get me off topic again, Franco, or I will set you on fire."

Franco: "Ooooh. Threats of violence from the warrior! How cliché."

Franco: "Okay, you just sitting there staring at me is really creeping me out. Please forgive me. You were talking about integrity."

Me: "Once I have determined that my word does indeed have value, or I decide to start putting value into my word, suddenly, my exact words start becoming more important to me.

"Whether I had it or not to begin with, I transformed myself into a person of integrity. I decided that my words themselves hold value and are important. When I decided that my words held value and were important, I became very careful about any agreements I tied my word to (my word is my bond) and found myself avoiding trivial conversations.

"When I avoided agreeing to things that I was incapable of following through on without great distress in my life and began avoiding trivial conversations, the noise pollution of my own internal incessant chattering thoughts dissipated. Simply by deciding that I could always be honest with myself, I eventually achieved clarity of mind. When I achieved clarity of mind, finding my way out of the rest of my Complex-PTS insanity became much easier."

Franco: "That's like a cascading waterfall of healing!"

Me: "That's why they call them the steps."

Franco: "So, you found that in the book of Alcoholics Anonymous? Are you an alcoholic?"

Me: "I don't think so. Much of what they use to define an alcoholic doesn't apply to me. I don't struggle with alcohol. I did use it to numb a lot when I was struggling with Complex PTS and have been known to tie one on once in a while."

Franco: "But you've read the book and go to meetings. I've seen you go to them."

Me: "Yes! I love a good AA meeting."

Franco: "Why would you go if you don't identify as an alcoholic? I mean, why bother?"

Me: "Pfft, for the wisdom! Much like that one line I just read to you. That one sentence helped rescue me from my own Complex-PTS insanity. There is powerful wisdom in those rooms and some of the best people I've ever met in my life. Those are the most honest people on the planet, people who aren't afraid to admit that they are struggling. All that, and I get to watch miracles. Miracles happen inside those rooms. I have never been kicked out.

"All of these life struggles are interwoven and codependent on one another, which is another I like to frequent—CODA, or Codependents Anonymous. I've witnessed an individual unravel decades of lifelong suffering with a fifteen-minute conversation inside one of those rooms before. He literally transformed in front of my eyes, I could see it in his face as if a boulder he had been carrying his entire life suddenly dropped, and he saw his escape path from insanity. I go into the rooms and when I introduce myself, I just say 'I'm an adult child,' and I am always accepted. Essentially I am saying, 'I'm not God' by doing so, and that is acceptable."

Franco: "Nice."

Me: "AA was the first room I walked into and the first steps I took in my path of healing."

Franco: "Why? I thought you said you weren't an alcoholic."

Me: "Yeah, but I was a known heavy drinker and prone to suicidal thinking and tendencies. I had some severe mental and spiritual issues that I needed to understand and get on top of. I needed new distinctions in my thinking. All of that requires a sober mind.

"I was told that all of my problems and the solutions to those problems were inside of my own thinking, and I couldn't even comprehend that when it was told to me. I protested that sort of wisdom. I needed to get some sobriety under my belt so I could think through a lot of these issues with a clear and focused mind. Sobriety was paramount to my spiritual healing.

"I needed to go from hating myself and my life to enjoying them both. I had some serious work to do. I couldn't do serious work if I were getting loaded all the time. That, plus the spiritual awakening that I experienced at Save A Warrior was so profound I made a vow that I would do whatever Save A Warrior told me to do. The founder of the program took me under his wing and told me he wanted me to go through the 12 steps of AA. I said, 'But I'm not an alcoholic,' to which he responded, 'I don't remember asking you that question.' I'm so thankful I did. It gave me clarity of mind and complete power over alcohol, which admittedly was questionable in the beginning.

"With that sober mind, I then went into ACoA (Adult Children of Alcoholic/Dysfunctional Families, something I did completely identify with). I was able to integrate my childhood survival traits that I still had in play as an adult and causing havoc in my life. Since then, I've been through three additional 12-step programs. All of them have been awesome and given me more power in my life."

Franco: "So, you're a fan."

Me: "Absolutely. I host a few programs now and take people through the steps. I hosted one that met at the distillery."

Franco: "A 12-step program at a distillery? That must have been an interesting tour."

Me: "Hey, it worked. A lot of people say that program saved their life. Once I figured out the pathway out of my own insanity and my words became incredibly valuable to me, I didn't feel like talking about how to make vodka anymore. That seemed trivial to me. Certainly not when someone in the tour group is a veteran or first responder that was struggling with Complex PTS and possibly thinking of suicide.

"I'd tell them, 'I know a way in which one can go from suffering to leading a powerful life that one enjoys. It starts with getting some dry wood. Can't start a fire without some dry wood. Let's get you sober.' I would invite them to the meeting I was hosting.

"That's where the true power in life comes from, in giving stuff away. That's the spiritual law of abundance. Whatever I give away returns to me. When I give away healing, healing comes back to me, but you can't give away that which you don't have.

"I described this once using an analogy to an individual that came to the distillery who had a problem. He was a veteran who was running a program that helped other veterans struggling with depression, anxiety, and suicidal ideation after returning home from deployment. It was a very noble thing he was trying to accomplish, but he told me his struggle was that three of his members had committed suicide in the past year and a half, and he didn't know what he was doing wrong.

"I told him that in asking me that sort of question, he was exposing the solution. He asked me to explain myself and I said, 'The way you described the problem makes me think you are a truck that's stuck in the mud, who's trying to pull out other trucks that are also stuck in the mud. When you try that, you all just sink a little deeper into the mud together, which is what you are doing now. Possibly consider getting your own truck out of the mud first and up on some dry land. Then you'll be able to pop those other trucks out nice and easy.' He just nodded and left after that."

Franco: "Did he ever get his truck out of the mud?"

Me: "I don't know, that's not my business. One of the things I cannot control is how someone perceives the counsel of my words. I try never to give advice to people or tell them what to do; rather, I merely tell them what has worked for me. Whether they follow those suggestions or not is entirely up to them. If you have what I want, I have to do what you did to get it. That, or rob you.

"I tell people, 'I follow the other warriors on this path before me as long as they have something that I want. By something I want, I mean I look at you and see sanity, sobriety, life, confidence, peace, and joy radiating out of you. You have it. I don't.

I want it, so I follow you and learn to do what you do. In that manner, we are all walking down the same path together.'

"There's an African proverb that says, 'If you want to go fast, go alone. If you want to go far, go together.' That's what we do, and that's what we do in all the rooms."

Franco: "Powerful. Anything else on integrity before we wrap up?"

Me: "Absolutely, thank you. Once I establish that I am now a person who places value in my own word and promise to never lie to myself, I almost become unstoppable. Deciding to have integrity is the most essential ingredient to living a rich, full, and powerful life that one enjoys.

Once I decide to have integrity, only then can I do an inventory of myself with honesty. It begins with a simple yes or no question. 'Does my word have any sort of value to myself, yes or no?' If the answer is yes, then I can ask myself more probing questions. Do I blame other people for the problems in my life, or do I take responsibility for them? Toward whom am I holding resentments, and how do I forgive them? Where have I caused others harm and either covered it up or ignored it? Stuff like that, but remember, I promised to be honest with myself when answering."

Franco: "You're talking about a moral inventory."

Me: "I am. The 12-step programs are spiritual programs, as is Save A Warrior. Me and every other living thing on this planet are spiritual beings. Depression, anxiety, and suicidal ideation are most often spiritual problems. When traditional medical treatment fails in those areas, it's most often because one is attempting to apply a physical solution to a spiritual problem.

"People often come to Save A Warrior after they have exhausted all other avenues of traditional medical treatment (usually at great financial expense), giving us the nickname 'the last house on the block.' Those people are usually dumbfounded when they leave. 'This is free? I spent $90,000 on other treatments for my PTSD, and you just gave me the solution to my suffering for free and in three days!'

"It's free to them, of course, but it's not free. We exist on the donations of generous people who care."

Franco: "Why not charge? Everyone else does."

Me: "Because then it becomes a transaction. What sets people free is simply sticking to the truth, doing a searching and fearless moral inventory of themselves, and taking responsibility for their part in their own suffering in life. I clean my side of the street in my life and in my relationships. That means I have to offer forgiveness when I'm holding resentments and make amends when I know I need to. Those things are keeping my brain constantly triggered by events in the present moment and drifting into depression and anxiety. Depression and anxiety are the stuff I constantly want to numb, driving me into compulsive behaviors, gambling, sex, drinking, or whatever. The moral inventory alleviates those compulsions."

Franco: "Then why don't more people do it?"

Me: "They might be ignorant of the wisdom, in denial, lazy, or they think it's working for them. Sometimes, even if they aren't enjoying life, they think, 'That's the devil I know, and I think I can keep managing it.'

"Sometimes if people come to me saying they are suicidal, I just tell them they have a language problem."

Franco: "*Pfft*. A language problem?"

Me: "Yeah, I tell them they're not really suicidal, they have a language problem, they're using the wrong words. If they were truly suicidal, they would have committed suicide before they came to me. They came to Save A Warrior because they are seeking a solution to end their suffering and actually enjoy their life. If they were truly and thoroughly enjoying their life, thoughts of suicide would never enter their mind."

Franco: "What's the response to that?"

Me: "Usually, they completely agree with that statement, and then I'll ask, 'What other language problems exist in your thinking? You are starved for wisdom.' The world has all the data it could ask for on the cell phones in our pockets, but completely starved for wisdom.

"Wisdom is what aids the spirit, not data. Data is for the physical world where there are problems. There are lots of problems out there. Use data to solve those problems, but never stop seeking wisdom. I am a spirit having a human experience. Wisdom resolves the problems going on in here, inside the meat puppet. In here, I can use wisdom to adjust my perspective to that world out there, and a lot of those problems out there just disappear like magic."

Franco: "No shit!"

Me: "No shit."

Franco: "No, I mean, this dirt is a little dry. How about one of those plant food spikes the next time you water me?"

Me: "I'll look into it."

Birds

The blue jays and cardinals are chilling out together on the feeder.

Franco: "I think humans could learn a thing or two from the birds. If the different varieties of birds can get along so well, why is it so difficult for humans?"

Me: "Because birds don't blame each other for their problems in life."

Franco: "He who blames his problems on others extends his own suffering."

Me: "Right you are. Humans tend to do that. Birds do not. Sue and I have taken to meditating on the back porch in the mornings, listening to the chorus of birds. There are dozens of varieties to listen to. Throughout the day, I often pause to notice if I can hear them or not.

"If I can hear the birds, that means I am focused on this present moment, and I will experience more peace in my life. I'm focused on the reality of this moment. If I can't, that means I'm lost inside my own head, focused on the insane noise pollution of my own internal thoughts, usually either dwelling in the past (depression) or predicting the future (anxiety)."

Franco: "Peace is always at 'right here, right now.'"

Me: "Those are its exact GPS coordinates."

Awareness of Spirit

When I became aware of my own spirit, that shifted my entire life experience suddenly.

I became aware of who I am inside this meat puppet, and it's as if I suddenly became aware of an entirely different universe. It's as if I were suddenly just born in that universe, and it was my first day. It was very exciting, and I was filled with wonder, just as I was when I was born in the physical universe.

I became aware that there was the universe that I already knew of on the front side of my eyeballs. Now I was instantly aware of the universe on the other side of my eyeballs. I was actually the ball of energy that was animating this meat puppet. That was my spirit. It resides here, in this universe inside me. The ball of energy that is me had only been focused on the world on the front my entire life. That universe had its set of rules to live by and its commerce system of rewards to adhere to.

Here, in the spiritual realm, the rules were very different. The things that were important in life, along with what was not significant, were almost completely different. In this new universe, I could be a very wealthy person. I merely had to redefine my definition of wealth.

Franco: "Well, that's rather convenient, don't you think?"

Me: "Franco, would you rather be right, or would you rather be happy? You may choose only one."

Franco: "I thought the two were connected."

Me: "That's an illusion in the societal thinking of the physical world. Often the two choices are in stark contrast to one another. The cult of culture we are raised in teaches us that we always want to be right, valid, and justified in all of our choices, lest we be shamed as a fool. Fear of shame thwarts finding true happiness. So which is it that you choose? To be right, or to be happy? If it helps, I will advise you that no one that has chosen happiness over being right has ever reported back to me that they've regretted making such a decision. See, the epiphany they discover after making such a choice is that when they find happiness, being right doesn't even matter.

"Here's another one. Would you rather have vast material wealth or internal peace of mind and heart? You can choose only one."

Franco: "I thought finding material wealth would bring me peace."

Me: "Again, they are often in contrast with one another. That's why Jesus said it's easier for a camel to go through the eye of a needle than for a rich person to enter the kingdom of God. I know a lot of incredibly wealthy people who are very miserable and continuously searching for peace. I also know a lot of wealthy people who jumped off the hamster wheel and have never regretted their decision.

"The measure of success out in the physical world is money, status, power, and stuff. Success out there is measured by acquiring things and believing the things will bring joy and peace into my life. That is confusing pleasure (brought by things in the material world and is brief in experience, never fully satisfying) with happiness (an emotion felt in the spiritual world that has a foundation of satisfaction). Nothing lasts long out in the material world. Once I acquire things out there, I now have to maintain and defend those things, causing anxiety.

"In the spiritual universe, the reward system is entirely different. Instead of acquiring material possessions, joy comes from giving, not receiving. Instead of accumulated wealth, the standard for success in the spiritual realm is measured in internal peace, joy, confidence, sanity, and freedom of choice.

"The truly remarkable thing was that even though that was my first day in that universe, the men who showed it to me already had all of that stuff and could show me how to get it. They had it. I wanted it. If I want what you have, I gotta do what you do in order to get it. They were absolutely willing to do that. Confidently successful people are always willing to share with others how they got that way. The amount of peace, confidence, and joy they possessed radiated outward from them.

"One of the first things that I had to do in order to be a success in this new universe was to get in tune with my inner feelings and emotions. Out there, in the physical universe, my meat puppet had nerve endings. The nerve endings either sent pleasure to my reception device (brain) or sent pain to it, letting me know when I was damaging the meat puppet. Internally, my feelings and emotions were my spiritual nerve endings.

"Out there, per one of the rules I had in the 'world according to Larry,' being in touch with one's feelings and emotions was considered to be a weakness or signs of weakness. It was even ridiculed. One would be punished in the household I grew up in if they expressed their genuine emotions. I learned to ignore feelings and emotions and simply buried them inside. Love was never expressed in our household. I invalidated most of my emotions so long ago that I had forgotten what many of them were. I was taught that as a child and followed that rule well into my adulthood. Most of the people I met in the veteran and first-responder communities I was a part of were doing the same thing, so it seemed like the correct way to be. By ignoring my internal feelings and emotions, I was actually ignoring my own spirit and invalidating that part of me, my true self.

"I also ignored depression, anxiety, and all the thoughts of suicide that were running through my mind constantly. Those are signs of a sick spirit, and those feelings just became normal. In order to heal my spirit from all the damage caused by ignoring spiritual pain, I needed to understand my own feelings and emotions. Out there, there was never enough stuff to satisfy me. I was always chasing more. That's the thing with stuff out there. The pleasure is always fleeting.

"In here, the spiritual universe, success was measured by peace and happiness. Once one acquires peace and happiness, how much money and stuff one has is no longer critical. It really depends upon which universe's rules one is following. I am either focused on the world out there or the world in here. I cannot focus on both worlds at the same time because the human brain cannot multitask. I was ignorant of my own spirit and invalidated my feelings/emotions for so long that I was utterly unconscious of the spiritual component of me. I was entirely focused on the material world for most of my life. Out there were all the problems I was trying to solve. 'The mind cannot serve two masters.'

"In the physical world, I was almost discouraged from pursuing spiritual success. The measure of satisfying 'success' in the material realm was always just out of reach. I lived as if I were a donkey following a carrot on a stick and was oblivious to it. Ironically, when I experienced success in the spiritual universe (which is obtainable), success in the physical realm no longer mattered. I found my spiritual awareness by following questions asked to consider by the warriors who came before me. They would ask a question out here, and I would have to go inside myself for the answer. Awareness didn't come specifically in one of the answers. It came simply by considering the question.

"In one moment, it dawned on me that the part of me from which I was getting the answers from was, in fact, my own spirit. I was being questioned about the shame and guilt I was carrying around. It's rather suspicious when one is carrying around the amount of shame I was carrying. To them, it was obvious. 'That person lacks spiritual awareness. Look at all that shame he's carrying!'

"To them, it was as if I were shoplifting a grocery cart underneath my T-shirt. It was very apparent that I was shoplifting. Meanwhile, I was acting like I wasn't shoplifting an entire filled grocery cart under my shirt. That was a rule to follow in the physical world: 'Just deny that you are hiding shame.' If you deny that you're hiding shame out in the physical world, no one ever calls you on it. They can't. They're all hiding their shame too. So, out there, the unwritten rule is, 'Don't point your finger at my bullshit, and I won't point out yours.' That rule didn't work with these men who had spiritual awareness. They were quite persistent.

"'Are you sure you're not hiding a shopping cart underneath your T-shirt? Because we can see it. If you wish to deny that you're hiding shame, can you possibly explain why your stomach is so bulky and rectangular-shaped?'

"Eventually, I just lifted up my shirt and showed them the shopping cart of shame. I've always had it underneath my shirt because I never knew what to do with it. When I showed them, they just said, 'That's what we thought,' and took it all away. When they just took it away, it was such a relief! I was ecstatic. 'I'm free of it! I've been hiding that shopping cart and dragging it around with me for over forty years!'

"I suddenly became spiritually aware, but they warned me to stay on the path they put me on. If I strayed from the path, as soon as I went back to the physical world, I would be tempted to hide another shopping cart under my shirt and start filling it with shame again. 'Because that's what they do out there! They hide their shame instead of dealing with it. Stay on this path, and you will find lasting joy, peace, happiness, and full self-expression.'

"I stayed on the path, did the work that they told me to do, and eventually found a well of love springing up inside my own heart. That's like the Cadillac of spiritual emotions. Once one finds the well of love that's inside them, nothing out there really compares to it.

Hypervigilance, Neuroplasticity, and the Gratitude Challenge

Me: "I'm often speaking to people who are experiencing various degrees of depression."

Franco: "I know. I'm sitting here eavesdropping on all the calls."

Me: "I wasn't talking to you."

Franco: "Well, you're talking to me now."

Me: "I'm just gonna set you outside for a bit so you can get some sun."

Franco: "Hey..."

Me: "Anyway, I'm often speaking to people who are experiencing various degrees of depression and cannot seem to get out of the mental funk. As I've come to find out, our human brains have neuroplasticity to them. That means they change shape a bit over time. If I were to take my brain out of my skull, it would look a bit like a head of cauliflower with a bunch of canyons and grooves in it. If you don't know this, uh, I don't know. Stop reading this and go look it up on the internet. That's what the human brain looks like.

"Now, I'm no rocket surgeon or anything, but the way the brain stores data is in various regions within all those ridges and valleys. Those ridges and valleys look the way they do based on the neural pathways that connect the data to different parts and regions of the brain. The whole thing is highly efficient and wired for survival. The brain organizes the data into different sections for efficiency, exactly like a personal computer does. It has sections for 'most recently viewed items.' It has sections for long-term memories. It has a short-term memory section. It does data analysis. It has sections that run programs in the background, such as breathing and heartbeat. It processes the electronic signals coming to it via the nervous system. It is a very high-tech, organic super-computer, and the whole thing is arranged, and it looks exactly the way it does right now to be as efficient as possible for the tasks it needs to perform.

"Human beings are also meaning-making machines. Every piece of data and memory that is stored in my brain has some sort of meaning attached to it. That is like the brain's internal Dewey Decimal System. That's how it keeps track of where it puts stuff. Imagine a library bookshelf filled with books, but each book has a bunch of labels attached to it telling you what the book is about. It might say that this particular book is a thriller or a comedy, perhaps.

"The experiences I have stored in my memory that I've felt shame about have little 'shame' meaning labels attached to them. So if I'm ever wondering why I'm such a loser, I can look through the shelves, and notice the labels. 'Ah, here's one. I got drunk at the Christmas party and flirted with a coworker. My wife didn't talk to me for a week. Right, I'm a piece of shit. We'll just leave that label on that piece of data and put it back on the shelf.' Things that have tremendous trauma surrounding them have their own labels. If I have Complex PTS, some of the labels on those pieces of data may read 'unprocessed.'

"The central processing unit of my brain is a gland called the amygdala. That part of the brain is definitely wired for survival. That's where my fight, flight, freeze, and fawn responses originate from. The amygdala responds to adrenaline. Whenever I experience something that causes an adrenaline dump, my amygdala swells up a bit. That's when I kick down the door and take care of business. When the situation is resolved, the adrenalin dissipates, and my amygdala calms down and shrinks until the next adrenaline dump. Then it swells back up again. It swells up, then back down. Up. Down. Up. Down.

"If that happens a lot (veteran/first responder/anyone getting up in middle age), my amygdala wears out a little bit or just stays in the on position. That's when I have hypervigilance. I just stay in fight/flight/freeze/fawn mode.

"This happens gradually, so I don't notice it as it's happening. It's like boiling a frog. If I throw the frog into boiling water, it will jump out. If I put the frog in cool water and turn the fire on low, it'll cook. That's the same principle that's going on with my amygdala.

"Hypervigilance just kind of creeps up on a person. You might notice that you have it if you are uncomfortable in crowded places or always have to sit with your back to a wall in a restaurant. If I can't leave the house without two guns and three knives on my person somewhere, there's a good chance my amygdala is stuck in the 'on' position. I think that it's okay when I'm that way because I think I'm just being wise, safe, and street-smart. 'I've seen a lot of violence. I've seen what happens to unarmed people.' I justify being that way.

"Remember, humans always want to be right, valid, and JUSTIFIED, so I make excuses for my behavior. Meanwhile, there is no peace in my life, and I can't seem to enjoy life. The hypervigilant person ignores that. Peace of mind and enjoyment of life seem trivial when compared to survival for the hypervigilant person.

"Remember, the brain is wired for survival, so the other thing the brain and amygdala are doing is looking for disasters down the road. It's always making 'worst-case scenario'-type predictions and catastrophizing everything. It's looking at life and making doomsday scenarios to avoid. It's making predictions. It's predicting, 'I'm gonna get divorced.' 'I'm gonna get fired.' 'I'm gonna go to jail.' 'I'm gonna get sick.' 'I'm gonna be homeless.' 'I'm gonna die.' 'I'm gonna be abandoned by my family/coworkers/friends.' It makes these doomsday predictions, and then I go about life trying to offset these doomsdays or control them somehow.

"The vast majority of the doomsdays my amygdala predicts never occur, and I don't bother to notice that because I have hypervigilance. Like a frog in boiling water, the water has begun boiling, and I've failed to notice that. Being hypervigilant has become my 'way of being,' and my brain has responded accordingly. It has arranged itself in such a manner that it runs most efficiently as a hypervigilant person.

"Logic tells me that if I could predict the future with any degree of accuracy, I would be a gazillionaire by now, would have sidestepped all the traumatic things I experienced in the past, and wouldn't have time to read this book because I would be busy ruling the entire world. But who has time for logic in such a dangerous world, right?

"Here's a question for you, Franco. Where's the amygdala getting all the data to make these dire future predictions?"

Franco: "Uh, I dunno. I give up."

Me: "From my own past memories. The amygdala, being the CPU of my brain, also has a blueprint of every neural pathway running through my brain connected to the memory of every traumatic thing I've ever experienced because that's the sort of stuff it wants to avoid.

"While my amygdala is making dire future predictions that will never occur, in the background, it's researching every horrible thing I've ever experienced because that is the sort of stuff it wants to avoid. 'He who dwells in the past will have depression. He who dwells in the future will have fear and anxiety. Only he who can reside in this present moment will ever have peace and tranquility.' The hypervigilant person can expect to have severe depression and anxiety and have no idea why. I am speaking from experience.

"Meanwhile, things like love, peace, joy, and happiness are nonexistent because those only exist in this present moment. They do not exist in the past (just a story in my mind) nor in the future (an illusion that my brain generates).

"That is also one reason a hypervigilant person is constantly depressed (which they may be reluctant to admit because they have the admission of such labeled as a 'weakness' in the rules and 'codes of conduct' section). The amygdala keeps the memories of those events in the 'most recently viewed documents' section of the brain for easy reference of things to avoid in the future.

"It does the same thing with memories over which I hold resentments, so the amygdala can keep an eye out down the road for people who will screw me over in a similar fashion. Because they are in my 'most recently viewed documents,' I will find myself often dwelling on them. When I dwell on my past, I will focus on my losses in life, people, and things that I've lost over time. I will shame myself over my own behavior: 'I should've done this, shouldn't have done that, could've done that better.'

"I cannot change or alter things that happened ten minutes ago, let alone years ago, so my dwelling on the past is needlessly filling me up with depression and shame over things I cannot change and the future, as the amygdala predicts it is never going to occur. The first step in resolving this issue is always simply admitting that there is a problem. Until that occurs, the hypervigilant person will never alter their mentality. Drugs can target the amygdala and offer limited relief.

"The long-term solution is to process past traumas properly. That means mourning things that haven't been mourned. Most hypervigilant veterans and first responders never feel entirely at ease with a civilian therapist because there is a lack of trust. There's a lack of kinship. Because of that, many say they never feel as if they can let their spiritual barriers down enough to fully process grief.

"There's the whole 'The sheepdog does not bother nor concern itself with the thoughts and opinions of the sheep' rule in the mental 'code of conduct' that often goes unacknowledged, and also, trauma, in order to be processed, has to be shared with someone who has earned the right to hear it. I'm not saying those thoughts and beliefs are pretty, but they are real, and many veterans and first responders hold them.

"When a veteran/first responder feels safe (in the company of other veterans/first responders) and is shown how to grieve appropriately, the trauma leaves the body in the form of tears. The human body relieves itself of trauma through tears.

"Once grieved, the individual experiences tremendous relief, the 'unprocessed' label is removed from the stored data, and the item makes its way out of the 'most recently viewed documents' section of the brain. Depression and anxiety become noticeably less severe afterward. That's been my experience, anyway."

Franco: "And then, everything is fine afterward?"

Me: "No. Oh, hell no. Rome wasn't built in a day! There is still the issue of the brain being structured for maximum efficiency to be in a hypervigilant way of being. There are issues of neural pathways being arranged and created in such a way out of habitually doing things the same way for decades, hiding shame, and so forth. It took decades to create the structure and neural pathways in such a manner to store trauma and be hypervigilant. It will take some time to change the neuroplasticity and the geographical outlay of the brain."

Franco: "I'm sure you have some suggestions?"

Me: "Indeed I do. First and foremost, building a daily routine that includes mindfulness meditation is critical. The meditation technique specifically targets the amygdala and, over time, can reset it back to a somewhat normal state. There is a ton of research to support this.

"I prefer the Warrior Meditation® technique because that's what I had been trained on, but I believe many mindfulness-based meditation techniques increase the neuroplasticity of the brain, making it more malleable. There are a ton of other scientifically proven health benefits to doing so. It increases cognitive functions, decreases blood pressure, increases memory, reduces age-related brain degeneration, and a whole lot more. My recommendation is to meditate daily, multiple times a day. And then, to actually change the neural pathways, what I often recommend to people is what I call the gratitude challenge.

"If I've been struggling with unprocessed trauma and hypervigilance, then my brain is designed and structured for maximum efficiency at looking for 'worst-case scenarios.' I want to change that, so what I often recommend is that while meditating daily, the person also does the gratitude challenge. The gratitude challenge involves making a commitment to write one person a 'thank-you' note every single day for ninety days to a year. I recommend holding oneself accountable to another person while doing this so the integrity of your word keeps you from quitting early.

"The challenge is very simple. I have to write one person a note thanking them for something they have done for me that has somehow blessed my life. I keep a list of the people I write the notes to so that I don't accidentally write the same person a thank-you note twice for the same thing (that can happen if I'm not keeping track). What happens is the first few notes that I need to write come to me very quickly. At the beginning of the challenge, there are multiple people who I can easily spot in my memories that I owe thank-you notes. After a while, it starts to become more complex. I find that I need to search my memory banks with a little more effort.

"I have found that the spiritual truth of 'he who dwells in the past will be filled with depression' does not apply when I am searching for gratitude. I don't know why that is, other than 'God likes me searching for gratitude.' Well into the gratitude challenge, I found it more difficult to find the people I owed notes to in my memory banks. Whether that's because I'm just shallow or I just ran out of people to write notes to doesn't matter. I still wanted to honor my word and keep true to my personal goal of honoring the gratitude challenge, so what I found myself doing was just keeping my eyes peeled for people I encountered throughout the day that I needed to thank for something nice that they did for me. Maybe it was a grocery clerk or someone I encountered at work. I found myself actively looking for gratitude throughout the day to honor my commitment. 'I'm a good cop. I always find exactly what I'm looking for.' When I look for gratitude, I find it!

"Soon, I finally understood the spiritual adage: 'To he who has, more will be given. To he who has not, even what he has will be taken away.' When I searched for and found gratitude, I suddenly kept finding more and more things to be grateful for. A person who doesn't have gratitude can only lose things. Thus, 'even what he has will be taken away.'

"With a combination of daily meditation (increasing the neuroplasticity of my brain) and the gratitude challenge, I changed the makeup of my brain from being a brain that's efficient at being hypervigilant to one that was efficient at looking for gratitude instead. I rewired and changed the landscape and the neural pathways of my brain from one that was efficient at looking for sadness and suffering to one that was efficient at finding joy and happiness. Obviously, after that, the way the world appeared to me and my perspective of life itself drastically improved. My days were soon filled with joy and blessings instead of depression and anxiety. I started experiencing happiness in my life. As an added bonus, I physically wrote and mailed my thank-you letters to the people I wrote them to."

Franco: "How did you find addresses for that many people?"

Me: "I'm just really good at finding people, let's say. I mailed my letters to them, and many of those people responded either by phone or wrote me back. The words they sent back to me often caused me to cry tears of joy. Some said that they happened to be at a very low spot in their lives, filled with depression themselves, when they received my letter unexpectedly. Some said the note was the nicest thing anyone had ever said to them and that it lifted them out of their depression. After speaking with them, some were moved to start gratitude challenges of their own, simply because my thank-you note impacted them so deeply."

Franco: "Awesome!"

Me: "Thank you. There, consider that your note for the day. The combination of meditation and the gratitude challenge improved my outlook on life so quickly that I still do it on occasion. I like to be in the habit of writing thank-you notes promptly now, but there are times when I will be in a funk for whatever reason. That's when I make another gratitude challenge and just chuck out back-to-back thank-you notes for a month or so. It never fails to pull me out of any sort of depression quickly."

Kindness Is Always an Option

When someone is struggling and still suffering, but still they try to help others, to me, those are the most extraordinary acts of love that I often witness.

And that is the parable of the widow with two coins in Mark 12:41–43.

You can help others right now, no matter who you are or where you're at in life, simply by being kind. Even when the universe seems to be crushing me, I can always be kind to others as a personal choice.

That might be my "two coins."

That doesn't mean I have to act inauthentically. I don't have to deny my own suffering to help you with yours. It just means today I might only have two coins, so "kindness" is my offering to the world.

And whatever I give to the universe always returns to me ten-fold, so kindness is a safe investment with a guaranteed return.

Franco: "Kindness is a choice."

Me: "Correct. So is being an asshole. Those are the sorts of decisions my spirit makes in any given situation. I often refer to my spirit as 'the little decision-maker inside the meat puppet.' I am the ball of energy that makes decisions about how I want the meat puppet to act. And then I make it do those things.

"I can choose to be kind, or I can choose to be an asshole. Those actions and the repercussions of those actions are my responsibility. Every action has a reaction. When I am aware of my spirit and am emotionally sober, I become an actor rather than a reactor."

Franco: "Basically, I do what I want."

Me: "Whether I am aware of it or not, I've been doing that all my life. I do whatever I want."

Franco: "What if you're in prison? You don't get to do what you want in there."

Me: "Even in prison, Franco, I do whatever I want. I have a choice of how I respond to the events occurring around me and decide if I wish to engage in them or not. Do I respond with kindness, or do I choose to be an asshole? I'm making that decision all day long, whether I am driving a car down the freeway or thinking about shanking someone in the prison shower. I control this meat puppet and how it acts. I take responsibility for my life and my actions, and that's it.

"When I am unaware of this, I can be overcome with the burdens of life. I think I have to manage so many things. Because my meat puppet is designed and wired for survival, what my amygdala (the CPU of my brain) does is predict future problems, offset those problems trying to manipulate the world and other people, so the problems I am predicting either don't occur or have some sort of beneficial outcome to me. When I am unaware, I will find myself attempting to control other people and things that are far beyond my control. I'm not God, so my tactics often fail, causing me frustration and exhaustion. I might lie awake at night, trying to sleep while thoughts of how to control the future run through my head. That's living in insanity."

Franco: "What's reality?"

Me: "Hold out your arms."

Franco: "I don't have arms."

Me: "Well, your leaf things, then. The only things I can actually control are within arm's reach of myself and within this present moment in time and space. That's it.

"If I want to enjoy a peaceful life, all I have to do is focus my attention on the things right here/now, within my arm's reach, and just be the best version of myself while I do that. I can scrape the rest of my life's burdens off of my plate. If I focus on just that and catch myself when I'm drifting my attention outside of that circle, I will have peace in my life, and my burdens in life will be light. That's called being present. I'm not telling you what to do, but I highly recommend being kind."

Franco: "Copy. I'll just sit here and be kind."

Me: "Kindness is infectious. I read a study in which people who witnessed acts of kindness in others were twenty-five times more likely to be kind to others themselves. It's very simple, but it's a decision I have to make. Do I act with kindness, or do I choose to be an asshole? Remember, the world I see is a reflection of who I am internally. If all I see are assholes out there, the answer as to why that's so is within me. If I want to see a kinder world, it starts by doing acts of kindness myself."

Franco: "Let the kindness revolution begin!"

Me: "Okay. Well, you're not going anywhere, so I doubt you'll be starting any sort of revolution anywhere soon."

Franco: "Watch me, you bipedal!"

Me: "Can I get you some water or something? You need to chillax. Simmadownnow.

"Now, although kindness is infectious for the greatest reward in the spiritual law of abundance, let no one see your acts of kindness. Those acts of kindness appear to others as miracles. Just be kind to be kind, and that spreads. Let not the right hand know what the left hand is doing. Consider doing an act of kindness and keep moving along before anyone else notices. People perceive such acts as miracles, and what's God do?"

Franco: "He performs miracles."

Me: "Correct. So when I'm out there acting like an undercover agent of God doing random acts of kindness and spreading the love that others perceive as miracles, essentially, I'm working for God. God likes to keep His workers fat and happy, let me tell you. The reward is a rich, full, and purpose-filled life full of peace and joy."

Franco: "So, do acts of kindness that others can see, or do them so no one can see?"

Me: "Try both, Franco. Just be kind."

Franco: "Dig it."

Relativity in the Here and Now

The amount of peace that I currently have in my life is directly correlated to the amount of distance I have placed between my current circumstances and where I am mentally dwelling "right here, right now." The further I get away from being mentally focused on this very exact moment, the more depression and anxiety I will experience, almost in direct proportion. The past equals depression, and the future equals anxiety. Peace is directly in the middle.

My present circumstances might not be pleasant. Right here, right now, I might be in a life-or-death situation. I've been in a few of those. I'll have adrenaline dumping as my amygdala figures out a path out of the current "danger." As long as I stay "present" in that situation, I will make better decisions and might actually survive.

In order to enjoy my life, I realized I had to constantly be mindful of my distance from "right here and now." I needed to keep my eye on it and be mindful of wandering too far away from it. That is something I had never paid much attention to previously. I had gotten to the point where I was suicidally depressed, and so I was open to making changes in my life. Wise people told me to mind my distance from the present moment in time and space and to keep it tight.

It seemed like an odd thing to be concerned about at first, but they had what I wanted (sanity, confidence, sobriety, peace, joy) and seemed to be thriving in life. If I want what you have, I've gotta do what you do in order to get it.

They recommended a daily practice of Warrior Meditation ®. The relief that it brought me was almost instantaneous. The daily practice of Warrior Meditation ® brought a calmness and peace into my life I had not experienced before. I have meditated every day since going into Save A Warrior in September of 2018, minus one or two days. Occasionally a day would arise in which my schedule was so hectic that I told myself I didn't have time to meditate. Those days sucked. They were so filled with stress and anxiety I vowed that I would never leave the house or speak to anyone again unless I had meditated that day first.

For me, it's as easy as a simple decision I make shortly after waking up. "Do I want to enjoy this day, yes or no?" If the answer is yes, I do want to enjoy this day, then I meditate. For me, it's a twenty-minute investment that reaps rewards for the rest of the day. I've seen others come through the Save A Warrior program, seemingly "get it," and transform their lives, but then later quit meditating for whatever reason, and their lives go right back to crap. I've seen that happen over and over to disastrous results.

Living with undiagnosed and untreated Complex PTS is living inside an absolute mental hell, isolated and alone in thought and being. Thoughts of suicide permeate every day, with some days being worse than others. I know I had Complex PTS and was suicidal for most of my life (no longer). I never want to go back to where I came from, not to that dark place of mental anguish. Thus, when the men who showed me the path out of it told me to meditate every day and never stop, I did what they told me.

I continue to meditate every single day, sometimes multiple times a day. My morning meditation is my favorite part of the day. When I do it first thing in the morning, that is like planting a flag and declaring, "I am taking charge of my day, starting right now, and I have decided that I am going to do everything in my power to enjoy it." My only goal in life is to be the best person I can put together each day. I have to meditate daily in order to achieve that goal.

I heard a wise person say that when one prays, that's talking to God. When one meditates, that's when God talks to us. I personally mix the two. I am often praying as I meditate. There is a verse in the Bible that I read when I was a small child that struck me in such a way that I underlined it and put stars next to it as if to indicate to my future self, "Hey, this is important!" That verse is Jeremiah 29:13, which states: "You will seek me and find me when you seek me with all your heart."

I underlined that verse and then spent the next half century searching for God as if He were somewhere up in the sky or hiding behind a tree somewhere. I searched for God in various

41

churches and religions. I never found Him. When I didn't find God because my sense of personal value was so low, I decided it was perhaps because He was disgusted with who I was as a person.

When I finally looked inward toward my own spirit and my own heart (there's a hint as to where one should look right there in the verse), I finally found God, and He wasn't even hiding. God is in the heart of all humans.

In my meditation, I recite a mantra. Basically, I say the same thing over and over inside my own head as I focus on tapping my fingers or focusing on my breath. My mantra is "Ah-vah." What reciting the mantra throughout the meditation does for me is it exercises my own spirit's voice over the noise of the thoughts running through my brain. When I say "Ah-vah" internally, it's like grabbing the microphone and speaking into my meat puppet's internal PA system.

The other day I was at the grocery store and wanted some ice cream, but the ice cream aisle was blocked with a barricade for some reason by the store. They had it purposely blocked with shopping carts for reasons I was unaware of. Sue and I paused and evaluated the situation.

"The ice cream I want is behind that barricade," I told Sue.

"They probably have it blocked for a reason," she responded.

I personally couldn't see the reason. I only saw that the ice cream I wanted was behind the barricade.

I said, "Yeah, well, *pfft*," and moved one of the shopping carts so I could get to the ice cream.

As soon as I opened the door and grabbed the ice cream, I could tell it wasn't as cold as it should be. The container seemed a little squishy, but I grabbed one anyway. After I returned to the cart with the "heisted treasure," I high-fived Sue, replaced the barricade, and said, "I'm a moonshiner at heart. I always leave the crime scene looking like it never happened!"

Just then, a voice came over the PA system, "Attention, shoppers! The frozen food section is temporarily closed for repairs! We apologize for this inconvenience."

"You know they're absolutely talking to you, and specifically *you*, right?" Sue asked.

I said, "Yeah, well, how about that? I'm *somebody* now, and the whole store gets to hear the story of the great ice cream caper in aisle 27. You and I are the stars of that show. I guarantee store security is at least watching us now, saying, 'Look at that fat dumbass. Keep an eye on him. See what else he does.' We should probably just check out and leave."

Internally, that voice that comes over the loudspeaker telling me to get out of the ice cream aisle is what I am doing when I recite my mantra during meditation. When I recite the mantra, it distinguishes my authentic voice from the noise of all the other thoughts and voices running around in my head. I am not the thoughts. I am the one listening to the thoughts.

I am is the person who occasionally grabs the microphone and speaks over the internal PA system and says, "I probably shouldn't be judging that person. They are just another human being trying to find happiness and end their suffering too, just like me. Maybe if I stopped judging them, I could help them."

I hear thoughts casting judgment in my head, I disagree with them (catch myself catching myself), and then recite what I believe to be spiritual truths to myself over the internal "loudspeaker." "He who blames his problems on others extends his own suffering."

I was telling my fellow traveler, "I talk to myself all day, reciting spiritual truths. Sometimes I say them out loud to myself. I probably appear as an insane person to others."

It's very important to commit certain spiritual truths and sayings to memory and, as I say, write them down in your heart. They then become the filter that I see life through and often prevent me from making serious mistakes in my "gameplay" of life.

I often feel a bit worn out as the day progresses. If that happens, I often take a short break and meditate again after lunch. Meditation brings my peace back to me.

I myself prefer the Warrior Meditation ® technique because that is what was taught to me. Occasionally I will just follow a guided meditation online or use an app on my phone, but Warrior Meditation ® is my preferred technique. There are other techniques out there. Warrior Meditation ® is a mindfulness-based style of meditation. I will include a chapter explaining the technique later in this book.

The whole point of meditation is to get one to focus on their exact position in time and space. That's why it brings so much peace. When one is mentally focused on the air entering and exiting their own lungs, that's about as close to "right here, right now" in time and space as one can get. The practice grounds me into this present moment, and then I go about my day seeing "What's next!"

Whatever is next will most likely start bringing my focus away from this present moment. Whether it's an email, a text message, or someone just walking up saying, "Hey, did you hear about ___?" As soon as they say that I am no longer "here," I am now mentally dwelling on whatever they are drawing my attention toward.

I keep my eye on the here and now, however, and bring my focus back to my breath whenever it's needed.

Other things that will pull me away from being present are my resentments and regrets. Those keep me mentally chained to the past, so I always want to get rid of them.

Neither resentment nor regret serves any purpose in the present moment and prevents the holder of such things from dwelling in the here and now. It's not good fruit to be carrying around. I highly recommend a 12-step program, and I don't even care which one. Preferably make it something relatable to something you may actually be struggling with. I've been through the steps of various programs eight times now.

They're all excellent, and the people I meet in those rooms are some of the best people I've ever met in my life. They're all good people who are working to improve themselves, are sincere, and most of them are paying their lives forward by taking others through the steps.

Some of the programs I've been through don't even relate to anything I happen to be struggling with, and I still get tremendous value out of going through the program and attending meetings. I gain so much wisdom in those rooms.

Going through a 12-step program helped me let go of a lot of resentments and regrets. Those are anchors to the past (where there is depression), and when I freed myself from their chains, two magical things happened to me.

I was able to let go of some of my past, and a lot of depression instantly vaporized out of my life. So depression disappeared. When I let go of it in my past, my mind quit predicting more of it in my future (where there is fear and anxiety), and I suddenly started feeling less anxiety in my life. Anxiety disappeared.

Without spending my mental energy focused on all this crap from the past and future, I was able to spend it more focused on this present moment (where there is peace).

I was explaining to my wife today, "Another thing that keeps me from residing in this present moment is being worried about what other people think of me. Now I'm not being present in my current position in space. When I find my value in the eyes of others, I'm now mentally focused on what the other person is thinking about me. I'm not dwelling here. I'm dwelling over there."

When I find my sense of value in the eyes of others, I'm not mentally focused on my own internal feelings and emotions. I'm more focused on yours, trying to decrypt them and manipulate them so that your eyes see me in a favorable way and don't cast judgment. Fear of shame creates an atmosphere in which I'm finding my value in your opinions of me, not my opinions of myself.

I'm not even being authentic when I do this. I am so mentally focused on you, because at one point, I was taught to do that by my upbringing and the society and culture I was raised in. I was told it was so important to have other people's respect and be in positions of power because "that's what the world liked." The social norms that I have been taught to believe and adhere to since birth are being right (avoid being wrong), valid, and justified. I want to win to avoid losing and dominate in order to avoid being dominated. These are the "rules of life" I trained to follow by my culture, social groups, religious organizations, and family in order to avoid feelings of shame and judgment. Fuck all that...

When I find my sense of value within myself, I start making investments in it, and those investments do have dividends. The dividends are that I start liking my life more and more. I'm living life for me, not you, and primarily focused on the things I like regardless of what others think of those activities. I am no longer seeking your approval, so I am now free to do whatever I please. I have freedom of choice returned to me when I make that adjustment. Life is better that way, at least I think so.

Other things that will keep me from being present are my opinions, preferences, and desires. The voice inside my head that never shuts up, telling me when to be pissed off, when to be offended, and when to be afraid, is fueled by my opinions, preferences, and desires.

I can't blame other people for my current perceived suffering because he who blames his problems on others extends his own suffering. The emotions I am experiencing are inside of me. Therefore, they are my responsibility to contend with.

In order to experience peace in my life and deeply enjoy this present moment that I am experiencing right now, I have to be able to accept whatever the present moment happens to be. My opinions, preferences, and desires cause me to want to change whatever I am experiencing right now. They cause me to want to impose my will upon the world to change whatever it is. I found when I do that, the change I am desiring is often less fulfilling than anticipated, is not satisfying, and now I want the thing behind the thing that I wanted in the first place.

The pleasure gained from anything in the physical world is fleeting. It doesn't last long, no matter what it is. A new car, a new house, a new relationship. In a very short amount of time, the new car becomes "the car," and the new house becomes just "the house."

Warrior Village has a ridiculously beautiful view of a private lake outside its wall-sized windows. I saw an individual who has been there many times standing at the window, staring out at the lake recently. I followed his gaze and noticed he was looking at a few geese that had just landed. I walked up, stood next to him, and said, "You've already forgotten how beautiful it is as you look at those pesky geese."

He instantly smiled and said, "You know what? You are absolutely right! The lake is gorgeous!"

We spoke briefly about how the human mind is struck by beauty the first time it registers something as "beautiful," and then whatever it is that stunned us instantly gets cataloged into the things that "just are," and we are no longer "struck" by the beauty. We get used to it.

After that, we just have to be present and almost force ourselves to notice the beauty. Our minds skip over that detail, starting with the second time we view the same thing twice. The same can be true of anything in the physical world. It's never as cool the second time around. The novelty is gone.

I heard a wise person say that in order to shut off that voice inside my head, I want to construct my life so that I am making far fewer "decisions." That's what the voice in my head is talking about: "This shouldn't be like that. It should be like this. How do I get this to turn into that? It's probably that person's fault that this is like that! It's certainly not my fault. I prefer this to be like that!"

I am deciding that I don't like whatever it is, or I think it could be improved somehow, according to my opinions, preferences, and desires.

When I have an opinion or preference, it limits the amount of joy that comes into my life and instead creates stress because now I have to defend my opinion (humans want to be right/ valid/justified, avoid being wrong).

Once I have an opinion, I now have to pay attention to my opinion and defend it instead of just enjoying whatever is going on for what it is.

I once got into a long debate on what band was better, Van Halen or Metallica. Both of them were incredibly awesome bands (but we all know Van Halen is far superior, right?).

My opinions, preferences, and desires cause me to judge other people whose opinions, preferences, and desires are different from my own. I often judge those people as "subpar" and thus bring negativity into my life experience.

When I find myself comparing Metallica to Van Halen, Metallica is at a severe disadvantage. The opinion behind which I'm casting my judgment is based entirely on my personal past experiences.

What Metallica doesn't know is Van Halen happened to be the very first concert I ever went to. I was sixteen years old. I couldn't believe my mother allowed me to go! What my mother didn't know was that my friends and I scalped an extra ticket to a prostitute who snuck marijuana into the show and sat right next to me the whole time.

From my vantage point, Van Halen rocks! The whole experience left a great impression in my brain as "awesomeness!"

So that's what Metallica is fighting against when I see them in my forties and think, "They're not as good as Van Halen."

Of course they're not! They're not going to make me sixteen years old again and sit me next to a prostitute who has weed.

Meanwhile, I'm casting judgment (based on my opinions, which are based on my past experiences) and not enjoying Metallica for who they are, which is one of the most incredible bands in the history of music.

Then we saw Rush, and...

Franco: "Rush is awesome! 'Modern day warrior, mean mean stride, today's Tom Sawyer mean, mean pride!'"

Me: "Roger that, my little soft-petaled cacti! My opinions, based on my past, are what prevent me from noticing the awesomeness that is happening in the present moment.

"I noticed that when I reduced my opinions, desires, and preferences, my enjoyment of life increased immediately. I was more present in the current environment, and instead of looking for what I didn't like or how I would change it, I was looking for all the things I liked about it instead.

"And I'm a good cop. I always find exactly what I'm looking for. If I'm looking for good things, I find good things. If I'm looking for ways things suck or could be improved, I will find that instead. I always recommend people start looking for gratitude. That is something I sometimes have to force myself to do. I always find it, but I have to look!

"I once told my mentor/fellow traveler, 'I know that whatever I give to the universe returns to me; thus, I am going to be doing an examination on myself and keeping an eye out for when and where I am judging others so I can put an end to it.'

"My fellow traveler, who has had many more years in recovery than I, simply said, 'Well, good luck with all that. Let me know how it goes.'

"A couple of weeks went by, and when I checked back in, my fellow traveler asked, 'So, how's all that, keeping an eye out for when you're judging others' thing going?'

"I said, 'It's maddening! As I've come to find out, judging others seems to be what I do all day. It seems to be my main thing! I judge everyone all the time for everything they say or do. There's no bottom to that well, no end in sight!'

"He said, 'I know. Me too. I judge others constantly.'

"The more I practiced, keeping myself aware simply by noticing, I discovered that I would judge others for even the slightest behaviors non-stop, all day long. It seemed impossible to stop myself. No matter how hard I tried to stop myself, I seemed to be judging others seemingly unconsciously and merely catching myself mid-judgment.

"At first, this seemed disheartening until I kept practicing. As I prayed about this flaw of character and kept a watchful eye out on myself, I noticed that at least I started becoming more aware of when I was judging others. I would catch myself as soon as I cast judgment on someone.

"An example of the mental conversation I would have 'Boy, look at that dumbass over there! They certainly are addicted to their own significance. What an asshole! Oh, there I go, judging them. If you spot it, you got it. But by the grace of God go I, forgive me.' I would then immediately reel my judgment back in.

"Once I judge another as being inferior to me (usually based on nothing more than my opinions, preferences, and desires), I am now less likely to be open to any wisdom they may hold for me. Their wisdom might be incredibly valuable, but I'll never know because, mentally, I have labeled them as an idiot.

"Let's say I have mentally labeled someone or a group of someone's 'idiots' because they are Democrats, and I am a Republican, or vice versa. I was most likely taught that those people were idiots by my parents or heavily influenced by the associates I surround myself with (school/work/social groups).

"Because I am constantly surrounded by these people, they are constantly espousing their opinions on things in my ear, and whether I admit it or not, I'm listening to them. I like to think I'm weighing those opinions to be true or not, but if a human hears one thing constantly, they tend to start believing it, even if it lacks truth.

"I've always tried to keep my political preferences to myself and avoid such discussions. If someone brings politics up, whether I agree with them or not, I forcibly change the subject. Sometimes they don't like it when I do that, and they walk away. That's just fine, and my life experience has improved!

"My ultimate spiritual goal in life is to have absolutely no enemies. Once I have no enemies, I no longer have to defend myself. The fastest way to have no enemies is to stop wanting shit from other people. Money, stuff, admiration, respect, acceptance, anything. Most of the people I considered to be enemies of any sort stood in the way of me getting something that I wanted, particularly from other people. 'That person doesn't like me now' or 'I'm not gonna get what I want because of you!'

"I'm blaming someone else (extending my own suffering/casting judgment), so now that person that I'm blaming, and possibly the person I want something from, is now my enemy. When I don't want anything from anybody, I avoid that entire scenario. I don't even have to deal with it.

"I am creating my future with the decisions I am making right now. I am the architect of my life experience. I have to make some decisions. That's what the human spirit does. It makes decisions. I often refer to my own spirit as the 'little decision maker inside of the meat puppet. The ball of energy that's animating the machine.' Now the chatter in my head is all based on the number of decisions I am making. If I can reduce the number of decisions I'm making (by reducing my opinions, preferences, and desires), the chatter dies down.

"When I learn to adjust my perspective enough that I have no enemies and view everyone as 'right,' there is no stress in my life. It helps to remember that we are all connected spiritually and that all humans are searching for happiness and an end to their suffering. All humans are doing that. All humans are searching for happiness and an end to their suffering. That's why all humans do whatever they do, whether I agree with what they are doing or not. Rather than judging them, I tell myself, 'That wouldn't work well for me in my gameplay of life.'

"They might have a different set of values that they are following in order to get there that does not coincide with my own. But I have made severe mistakes of my own in life. But by the grace of God go I. I also cannot predict the future. I don't know if the thing I am predicting that's going to bring harm in that person's life is actually going to lead to their salvation, and the act of me stepping in the way of it screws that plan up. I'm not God. I cannot predict the future. I judge a tree by its fruit. If I like the fruit that's on the tree, I get closer to that particular tree. If I don't like the fruit, I simply avoid the tree.

"When I try to not only manipulate that person's future, not only do I often fail (I'm a god with no power), but where am I not mentally focused? When I am mentally focused on someone else's problems and all the misery destined for their future based on my opinions, preferences, and desires, I am not right here, right now, where there is peace.

"Emotional sobriety is knowing that my feelings and emotions are mine to contend with, and yours are yours. When I am emotionally unsober, I am hyperaware of your emotions, and I'm trying to manage them via manipulation. I'm trying to cause you to have a favorable opinion of me. This might cause me to make your problems my problems so that I can fix your problems for you, causing you to look at me as if I'm a knight in shining armor or something. I might even ignore my own problems, feelings, and emotions as I'm fixated on yours.

That's called being codependent. It's why a lot of relationships fail, and there's a 12-step meeting for that (CODA).

"I was explaining this to a friend recently, and he said, 'I wish I could be inside your head just for five minutes to see what goes on in there.' I told him, 'You wouldn't want that. It's a zoo in there, with a lot of noise. There are constant thoughts that bounce around back and forth, like a busy mall. I can get lost in all of the chatter and noise. But then, every once in a while, I grab the microphone, get on the loudspeaker, and announce loudly, "You need to stop judging that person," or "That was a wildly inappropriate thought! Let's reel that back in or pick another topic. I have one for you! Seventeenth-century architecture, and go!" 'The thoughts are the chatter going on in my head. My spirit is listening to all the chatter and deciding if what it's hearing is true or false. I am not the thoughts. Spiritually speaking, I am the one listening to the thoughts. I can control my thoughts if I choose and talk over the loudspeaker anytime I want. I'm either focused on the world and listening to the chatter in my head, or I'm in here, noticing, focusing, and controlling my thoughts. The human brain cannot multitask, and the mind cannot serve two masters. I'm constantly going back and forth on what I'm focused on. Mentally, I am either focused on whatever is out here and listening to the thoughts or talking to myself as I catch myself catching myself. I heard a man describe his mind as the world's dumpster. One cannot control what experiences the universe brings into their life and imprints itself into their brain's memory banks. Those memories heavily influence the thoughts I have, and I have little control over that either. So being inside my head means wading through a lot of trash and pollution, and occasionally you'd hear me on the loudspeaker redirecting my mind's focus. He said, 'Holy crap! That's what is going on inside my own head too! It's the exact same thing!' I laughed and said, 'I know! That's how all human minds work! None of us are terminally unique, so as I describe how my mind works, I'm describing how most everyone else's minds work too.'

"Although I do not have control over what goes into the dumpster (which is my mind), I do have some control over the direction my ship is heading. I am the captain of this vessel, which is my meat puppet. I have some control over the people I choose to surround myself with and the activities in which I get involved. I have some control over the environment that I subject myself to.

"I heard a wise person once say, 'I can't change the people around me, but I can change the people around me.' When I surround myself with good people whom I aspire to be more like due to their qualities of character, their words are the things that go into my dumpster, thus becoming the thoughts bouncing around inside my head.

"It goes without saying that if I expose myself to lots of pornography, I'm going to have thoughts of a sexual nature inside my head constantly. If I surround myself with a barrage of political opinions, those thoughts are going to be the background noise in my head. Those are going to influence me. Whomever or whatever I choose to surround myself with is going to have a significant influence on the thoughts that permeate my thoughts and my perspective on the reality I am living in.

"If I surround myself with negative people who are constantly complaining, gossiping about others, and filled with drama,

I'm going to have a very negative view of life and the world. If I surround myself with authentic and happy people who are doing well and practicing good self-care on themselves, I'm going to be a happier and more authentic person myself.

"When I understand just how much our spirits affect the spirits and life experiences of everyone that comes into contact with me, it becomes my duty to unfuck myself as best I can so that I can bring as much joy into every interaction I have with other people as possible. If I can't bring a blessing, at the very least, bring no harm. That doesn't mean that I hide my problems, deny my emotions, or act inauthentically. That means it is my duty to focus some attention on my problems and correct them. I do the things in my life so that I can be of service to others.

"Remember, spiritually, it's much better to give than receive, and the spiritual law of abundance tells me that whatever I give to the universe returns to me tenfold. If I do no work on myself, I end up spreading misery to others. Misery returns to me. If I spread gossip, others are probably talking negatively about me (probably talking about what a horrible gossip I am). If I cast judgment, judgment returns to me. If I spread peace, peace returns to me. My world becomes more peaceful. If I cast joy, joy returns to me. It's a pretty simple concept, really. I am creating the world that I am living in, basically. The physical universe that I see is a reflection of who I am internally. If I don't like it, then I probably have some work to do on myself. I was once told by a very wise person, 'All of your problems, and the solutions to those problems, are within yourself.'

"The basic concept is if I surround myself with people who are doing well mentally, physically, and spiritually, I am going to be significantly influenced to do better myself because their words and behaviors are going into my mind creating the thoughts that my spirit is listening to. Quit hanging out with assholes, is the short version of all that.

"If I stare at a bright light and then close my eyes, I can still see the bright light for a little while. The light has caused an imprint on my eye's retina, which I can still see after the light has gone. My internal thoughts are exactly like that. My thoughts are the residual after-effects of my life experiences and the words of the people I have kept company with. Those thoughts become the background music of the house in which my spirit resides.

"Speaking of music, even the music that I play throughout the day echoes through my head long after I have shut the music off. I used to amp myself up by going to work with heavy metal music that had very violent undertones. In my tank, I would charge into battle while listening to 'Die with Your Boots On' by Iron Maiden or drive into work on the raid team listening to 'Let the Bodies Hit the Floor' by Drowning Pool. Later, I would be doing anything else, just walking around, and the lyrics would still be playing in my head: 'If you're gonna die, die with your boots on! If you're gonna try, stick around. If you're gonna cry, just move along.'

"I guess that was pretty good background music for someone going into battle or raiding a crack house, but I probably wasn't the most approachable person for your average person. A person looking at me might have thought, *Boy, that guy looks like he will just murder everyone.* Meanwhile, I'm cooking a burger on the grill, humming along to 'Die with Your Boots On,' play-ing in my head.

"If I want to have peace in my life, one thing that helped me was control what influenced the background music in my head. I stopped listening to music that glorified violence. I stopped watching movies and TV that glorified violence. I stopped play-ing violent video games. I stopped watching the news (I don't need others telling me what I should be pissed off about; I've already got plenty on my own). When I stopped entertaining myself with violence, the world became vastly more peaceful and enjoyable to me very quickly.

"Early in my recovery, my mentor/fellow traveler asked how life was going for me. I described it as: 'It's like I'm walking on a tightrope. I have to focus very hard throughout the day. If I let myself drift and step to the left, I fall into the past and into depression. If I step to the right, I fall into the future and the pitfalls of anxiety. I just keep my eye on the ropeway ahead of me and keep walking forward.'

"I learned that there was seemingly an entirely different world available to me that I wasn't even aware of before if I could just keep my focus on this present moment. The world that was made available to me had vastly less stress. It was more serene and beautiful. Problems disappeared all by themselves.

"The stark differences in the way life and the world appeared to me when I was aware and fully present were astounding. It was as if I were on a different planet. It's obviously that same planet. I was just unaware of this world before because I wasn't focused on the present moment. I had no peace.

Instead, I always focused on the pollution of thoughts blaring in my head, predicting disasters in the future and trying to control them.

"That is the power of Warrior Meditation ®.Creating a daily practice that includes daily morning meditations was critical in my recovery. My decisions in life became easier and more accurate. My judgments of others fell when I indeed became present. *Spiritual bypassing* means I am doing something or engaged in some activity that prevents me from being focused on my own current spiritual perspective, thoughts, and feelings. I'm neither focused on my current circumstances nor my own spirit. It's almost as if time stops while I am engaged in whatever the activity is. I am negating my own internal perspective and doing something so that my focus is solely on the activity, and the world around me deadens and numbs.

"It might be alcohol or drugs. That's why they call hard liquor 'spirits.' I am bypassing my own spirit and creating an altered state in my mind in which I am not focused on my present circumstances. It might be shopping, binge-watching TV, playing video games, and even working out. Running. Porn. Eating. There are hundreds of ways one can spiritually bypass. Some of those things might not be bad, such as running, unless it's done intentionally to spiritually bypass and avoid focusing on one's own problems and issues in life. Moderation is the key to everything. If I can enjoy something in moderation, it will not cause me too many hurdles in life.

"I heard a wise person say I cannot selectively numb things in life. If I am numbing out pain, suffering, and misery, I am also numbing out joy and happiness. I might not even notice the things that bring me joy and happiness as they happen. My life will appear joyless to me because I have numbed everything in attempts to get rid of suffering.

"It says in the Bible that unless a person becomes like a child, they cannot enter the kingdom of God. I explained that to someone recently: 'The kingdom of God is not a destination out there somewhere. It is inside the heart of every person. It is not a destination to arrive at after death. It's here right now. Like every king, God is inside His kingdom. God is not out there, hiding behind a tree somewhere. God is inside the kingdom of God, which is inside your heart. To enter the kingdom, I have to let go of the things that I cannot let go of out here in this physical realm. I have to be able to let go of all the stuff out there, the resentments I hold, and my past experiences. I have to let go of my desires. I have to offer forgiveness in places where I once cast judgment. When I can confidently let go of this world, then I can enter the kingdom of God. When someone enters the kingdom of God, you can tell. They are instantly filled with joy. There is great beauty in this present moment. We just have to look for it and notice it. Judge a tree by its fruit. The fruit of God is joy. When someone finds that inside themselves, they are instantly filled with joy and wonder, just like a little child.'

"When I let go of opinions, preferences, and desires, peace and joy return to me. When I practice gratitude and throw gratitude out to the universe, my life becomes filled with things to have gratitude for. Jesus said, 'Seek first his kingdom...and all these things will be given you as well.' That means that when I start playing the game of life by seeking wisdom and applying it to my life, the concerns of the physical world negate themselves. It's true. That works."

Franco: "Hey, are you going to bring me back in on this chapter?"

Me: "No. Moderation is the key to everything."

Franco: "Ass."

Decisions

Me: "The world I am experiencing is built upon the decisions I've made in the past. The universe I see is a collection of things I've experienced and added meaning to. Just like the story of Adam in the book of Genesis, when he went around naming the animals, I did that same thing after I was born. In fact, if one looks at that as a fable instead of a verbatim historical document, it takes on a whole new meaning and turns into the story of every human being's creation. There was a parting of the seas (my mother's water broke). Dry land was created (each human's birth). There's the sun and the moon (the illusion of time added). And then each of us went around adding meaning to everything, essentially naming the animals. That more or less details the creation of the human mind and the human experience.

"We're all born without having a vote in the matter, we live in the illusion of time, and we go around adding meaning to everything, every person, and every experience we encounter. That mind is full of meaning. That is who I think I am when I believe I am a completely separate person from everyone else.

"Back that story up and notice it says that God breathed the spirit of life into Adam. And then it says God made Eve out of Adam and told those two to populate the earth. In the story, it doesn't mention that God had to breathe the spirit of life into Eve. In the story, she already had it when she was created from parts of Adam. When they had offspring, it doesn't say God had to go around breathing life into all of them. It doesn't say, 'Oh wait, I gotta go breathe life into that one, and that one, and that one!'

"If I am to follow the story of Genesis, the spirit of life in all human beings is more like a cell dividing and replicating by mitosis. In that manner, we are all spiritually connected. The same breath of life that was in Adam is the same breath of life that's in everyone. We are each an artist born with blank slates on which we begin painting. What we paint on the canvas is based upon the meaning we've added to all of our varying experiences. That's what gets painted onto the canvas. What I see on the canvas is a reflection of who I think I am, based on the meaning I've attached to everything in my mind. The fact that some people will read this and decide they don't like it or consider it sacrilege is wholly based on their own personal experiences in life.

"If I do not like the picture that I have painted on the canvas that contains the picture I call 'life,' to change it, all I have to do is examine the meaning I have attached to certain things. The world I am seeing in my life right now is entirely based on the decisions I have made in the past. I made those decisions based on the meaning I have attached to experiences. I can edit all of that.

"Just like this book, I can hit the backspace key, back up to an experience, examine it, process it, and change the meaning I had attached to that particular event. When I change the meaning, the entire picture I have painted on the canvas shifts into something different. If I think the picture looks like shit, it is within my power to change all that. I will have to examine my past in order to do that."

Franco: "I thought you said, 'He who dwells in the past will be filled with depression.'"

Me: "I didn't say that; I was quoting Confucius, and that is true. There is a way to examine one's past without being filled with depression afterward, however. Do it with the purpose of simply understanding oneself and in the company of other safe people. Perhaps try meditating afterward. When I do it that way, my past becomes reference material instead of a tragic tale of woe. It's more of a road map of how I got to where I am now.

"If I consider my life a miserable experience, once I separate the facts of what happened from the meaning I have wrapped around the facts, I notice that all of the depression isn't in the actual facts. The depression is in the meaning I have attached to those facts. I can separate the two, almost holding them in opposite hands. I can drop or adjust the meaning at my leisure. When I drop the meaning I have attached to the story of what happened, I'll notice I just dropped all of my depression also."

Franco: "That sounds like, well, that's just a lot to wrap my leaves around."

Me: "You're attempting to add meaning to what I just said. Gotta catch yourself catching yourself.

"Here is what helped me at the beginning of this process of fixing the painting I call 'my life.' I am the artist. I am the one painting the picture that I see of the world. The world I see on the canvas is made up of things that I know that I know and things that I know that I don't know, all mushed together. Those are the things that I know and know that I don't know about. Those are the only things that I can attach meaning to; thus, that is the universe I see out there on the front side of my eyeballs."

Franco: "That sort of makes sense."

Me: "Okay, let's try this. Things that I know, for example, I know how to make booze. I own a distillery. And I know how to shoot guns. I've had a long career in the veteran and first-responder communities. Those are the things that I know that I know. Things that I don't know, for example, after I shoot the gun, I don't know how to clean the damned thing well enough to get it past the armorer on the first try, and I don't know how to make a cheesecake. I know that I don't know that. Smoosh all of that stuff together, and that is the universe as I know it."

Franco: "Got it."

Me: "Who I think I am as the artist who's painting that picture is my role in that universe made of the things I know and don't know about."

Franco: "Tracking."

Me: "My role in that universe is based upon the meaning I have attached to the experiences I have encountered in that universe and formed opinions about whether I liked those experiences or didn't like those experiences. In my human way of thinking, that is who I think I am. I am a collection of past experiences and meaning that I have attached to those experiences. When I realize that it's entirely based on the meaning I have attached to those events and that it's all malleable, I can reinvent who I think I am any time I choose."

Franco: "Simply by changing your opinions?"

Me: "No, by changing the meaning or removing the meaning attached to the event altogether. Opinions are like assholes."

Franco: "Yeah, everyone has one, and they all stink. You've said that before."

Me: "The fewer opinions I have in life, the more peaceful and enjoyable life experience I will have. Trust me on that. Life can just flow easily without my opinions getting in the way of it all. Who I think I am is based on my role in the universe that I know of. My role is based on my opinions, preferences, and desires. There are things that I like and dislike out there in the universe.

"How I perform my role is based on a series of rules I have created to abide by based on my opinions, preferences, and desires. This is the world according to Larry, the rules of life. That is my 'Larry's Code of Conduct.' These are the rules I live by and try to conform to so that I can impose my will out there on the universe, in other words, what I am attempting to paint onto that canvas that's in front of me. I need to be mindful to stay on my canvas.

"Imagine if we are painting together, side by side, and I glance over at your canvas and try to alter it. I don't like that tree you have painted by that stream or something, and I just reach over trying to adjust it for you. Maybe while you leave to go to the bathroom, I will just reach over and paint a building where you had painted a tree. How would you feel when you came back from the bathroom and saw my adjustments to your painting of a natural landscape?"

Franco: "I'd be pissed off! You just painted over my cousin, Phil!"

Me: "Right! That's the response I get from others when I attempt to impose my views and opinions on others. It leads to resentment and frustration for everyone around me if I keep doing that. You might yell at me, 'Stay on your own canvas!' That's to be expected. But that's what it's like when I try to fix other people. I can only fix myself. When I try to fix other people, it will always lead to resentment. When I stay on my own canvas and start making better decisions now, those decisions start appearing on the canvas in front of me.

"Be advised. I've noticed that I make my best decisions right now, in this present moment. If I try to make my decisions based simply on how I predict things will look in the future, it always leads to frustration. When I stay present, I start making better decisions. I'm making decisions to address problems as they're happening, making adjustments as they're needed instead of predicting how things are going to pan out in the future. Often I find that when I make decisions based on future predictions, sometimes I predict things wrong, and my 'solution' is now useless when 'now' catches up to me.

"When I focus on problems happening right now instead, I can see the results as they're happening, so I tend to make better decisions in life right now. Do you ever notice how one problem seems to be attached to another problem? That's what life is. It's a series of problems. When I start making better decisions at this moment in time, even the problems attached to them end up being better problems to have. The problems get better, and my whole life improves.

"I don't even hardly notice that my life is improving because I'm busy living it and seeing it from the vantage point of being in the center of it. Sometimes I do pause and glance (never stare) at my past just to enjoy the distance from a life of hell. I might decide in the future that I will want a tree in that spot on the canvas, so I start painting a tree. Then something happened in life, and suddenly I decided that I needed a mountain, exactly where I started painting the tree. Now I have to paint over the tree. I've wasted all that time painting the tree, and now I don't have a blank canvas to work on anymore. I have to paint over the tree, and some of it bleeds through. For the best-looking painting, it's best if I make my decisions mentally residing in the present moment.

"When I process the meaning I've attached to my past and understand myself, my mind will start to slow down on predicting the future, and I will learn how to paint (make decisions) in the present moment, and the life I am painting onto the canvas will just flow out of me. It makes for a much better-looking painting."

Self-Value and Worth

Me: "I struggled with low self-esteem for most of my life. I had an idea that I was worth less than dirt, and that was also something I hid from discovery from the rest of the world. I had an internal critic inside my head, constantly filling my mind with thoughts such as, 'You know you're an idiot, right? You're crazy. Beneath everything, you're still insane. You are a piece of shit. You're a loser.' It was a constant internal monologue that I struggled with. That constant internal beratement of myself drove me to present an alternate identity to the outside world, one that was more acceptable to others. I craved acceptance and approval from others.

"All humans do this. Humans are herd animals, and we are all born with the instinct of abandonment terror, and being outcast from the community at large. All animals have some basic instincts that they're born with. My dog, Jimmy, likes to be obedient, and for a dog is pretty intelligent. He has a large vocabulary (for a dog). If I tell him, 'Get on point,' he will stay fifteen to twenty feet ahead of me and to the left. He knows many verbal commands and even knows hand signals, such as holding a fist up for 'stop' and pointing a finger, indicating which direction I want him to go. He seems intelligent and usually likes to be obedient.

"However, sometimes on our perimeter sweeps, his instincts will take over, and he will get lost in a spot on the ground. Maybe another dog or animal had peed there. He will stop to do a full investigation, to the point that he will be disobedient and ignore my audible commands. He does this intentionally. I know he does it intentionally because I will be telling him, 'Jimmy! Get out of whatever that is,' and he will continue sniffing the spot while looking at me from the corner of his eye. That irritates me because I know he's being intentionally disobedient when he does that. He will keep sniffing the spot, neglecting his duties of being 'on point,' watching me walk closer and closer until I get within striking distance, and then he'll suddenly tear off in a sprint to get back 'on point.' I will mutter, 'Hey, ass, you're acting like a child!'

"Now, from his vantage point of being a dog, I might appear to be the ass, having no idea of the importance that this scent holds in his world. That pee spot might be some internal email messaging system created by animals thousands of years ago, and the message may contain information of incredible vital importance regarding the balance of the universe as we know it. I don't really know for certain. Maybe the earth will spin off its axis if he doesn't read and respond to that message by pissing back his response to it. What I do know is his built-in internal instincts to investigate random pee spots overruled his desire to be obedient at that moment. All animals have instincts. Birds migrate, bees pollinate, and so forth.

"Our natural-born instincts as humans are to never be abandoned. To a baby human, abandonment means death. A human baby is entirely dependent upon care from others for survival. Humans need to eat food in order to survive, and as babies, that food is provided by our caregivers. That's our most basic human instinct, the number one rule of life, on top of which we base all of the other survival rules we create as we grow. It's built into the innermost part of our brain, and our brains develop and grow around that one rule. We learn to seek the approval of others as children. It's a natural evolution of thinking. We all want to be accepted into the group and tend to become approval seekers. For children raised in loving homes, this abandonment terror dissipates as the child grows.

"For children raised with a dysfunctional parenting system (one or both of the parents is absent, an alcoholic, drug addict, or otherwise struggling with some sort of mental illness), the abandonment terror strengthens instead of dissipating, and the rules one then creates for gaining approval and acceptance can get chaotic. Trying to survive in such a household, my abandonment terror was reinforced as a legitimate concern.

"I then developed multiple childhood survival traits, tactics I learned to live by in order not to be abandoned by others. There are multiple layers of common survival traits. Lacking positive male role models and community, I continued to employ these survival traits well into my adult years. There wasn't a class in high school or the military to advise otherwise, and many of the survival traits were rewarded in my adult careers, reaffirming them to me as I was correct. That is how life works.

"Such as learning to dominate to avoid being dominated. One might think I picked up that characteristic in my chosen profession, but the exact opposite is true. I was drawn toward those professions due to my survival traits, and those tactics were rewarded in those careers. I'm not telling anyone else what to do, merely a suggestion that if anyone happens to kick down the front door of a gang-run crack house, I highly recommend that you start dominating immediately. I did, and all of my buddies on the raid team would basically congratulate me, 'Hey, great job! Way to kick ass and take charge.' That reinforces the idea in my head, 'This is the correct way to handle the entire life experience.' Be advised that's an excellent trait to have when raiding crack houses, but it's not great to have when trying to emotionally connect with one's own children.

"That's one of many survival traits. There are fourteen of them listed in the Laundry List Workbook of Adult Children of Alcoholic and Otherwise Dysfunctional Families (ACoA). (As of this writing, the organization is contemplating changing the title of that book/program to remove the word *alcoholic*). I do wish to discuss one of the most common traits that most people have at least some measure of in their ways of being. That is finding my sense of personal value in the eyes of others. We develop this trait directly due to our fear of abandonment and fear of being ostracized from the community at large. This is why we hide our shame (something all humans are guilty of) and develop nonshareable problems, which hamper deep spiritual connections with other humans. Our sense of personal value is so low we fear that if you knew me for how I view myself, I would be shunned. I learn to hide my shame (nonshareable problems), and turn into a people pleaser. I lose my sense of personal identity as

I learn to do and say other things just to get the approval of others and not be shunned.

"A person with this characteristic will do and say things not because they specifically want to but because they think the other person or group wants them to. Their main concern is not being shunned. Part of what I assumed responsibility for was how others saw me, what others thought of me, and their moods. This is also natural. Children assume responsibility for all that happens to them by default. People with this trait become hypervigilant for shame and judgment being cast toward them from the eyes of others. When I have this trait, what I think about myself is of no concern. I already know what I think about myself. My sense of personal value is incredibly low. My only concern is what other people think about me. My personal interests go ignored. What interests me are your interests, as I am constantly seeking the approval of others. 'We lose our own identities in the process.'

"All of this creates anxiety and dysfunction in my life as I exist powerlessly, unaware that I cannot control what other people think about me. Being codependent means I am attempting to control and manage your emotions and feelings so that they are always favorable toward me because I am terrified of abandonment. I will stay in relationships in spite of severe abuse. In doing this, I am also allowing the other person to control and manipulate my internal feelings and emotions. My happiness becomes dependent on their approval. This all leads to a joyless existence, void of any sense of personal self-expression."

Franco: "I assume you are going to get around to discussing a way out of this nightmare at some point?"

Me: "I was thinking about it. Maybe after I get back from the store. I'm gonna run a couple of errands. You need anything?"

Franco: "Come on, man!"

Me: "Fine. I'll keep writing. The first chip in the armor of that trait came when a person I respected as a mentor casually mentioned in conversation, 'What other people think about me is none of my business.' That statement landed on me hard because to understand what he meant by that, I had to look inward to consider if I was guilty of being concerned about what others thought about me. I examined myself and discovered that I myself was guilty of this behavior. Hell, I was concerned about what *he* thought about me when he said it, so obviously, I found myself guilty. 'What other people think about me is none of my business.' I had to write that down in my heart and repeat it to myself often.

"After thorough self-reflection, I found that almost all of the value I placed in myself I found in the eyes of others. I had placed almost no value on myself as a person. As always, admitting that I indeed had a problem was the first step in recovering from the problem. Having no value in oneself is a serious problem, particularly when one is struggling against suicidal ideation (a common trait in Complex PTS).

"To build value in myself as a person, I followed the path of those that had gone before me. At one point, I heard, 'The best thing I can do for the people that I love and care about is focus entirely on my own healing and make my own recovery the number one priority of my life.' I struggled with this statement at first and wanted to reject it mentally and spiritually.

Placing my needs ahead of everyone else seemed 'selfish' to me. I had spent my entire life placing the needs and cares of others ahead of my own. That is true of all veterans and first responders. We place the needs of our entire country ahead of our own, up to the point of our own deaths in the line of duty. Placing the needs of others ahead of my own seemed like the natural way to do things. I had to take into consideration that the people who told me this had never lied to me before and had my best interests in mind. Furthermore, they had what I wanted (sanity, sobriety, confidence, peace, joy). They had it. I wanted it. If I want what you have, I have to do what you do in order to get it."

Franco: "You've said that before."

Me: "I say that all the time. It's worth repeating. So I tried placing my recovery from Complex PTS as the number one priority of my life. I read the books they told me to read and attended the meetings they told me to go to. Actually, they told me to attend ACoA meetings regularly, and there weren't any around. This was all pre-covid, so internet-based meetings weren't a big thing yet. We couldn't find a meeting near us, so we started an ACoA meeting at the distillery."

Franco: "You started a 12-step meeting at a distillery? How did that go over?"

Me: "It went well, actually. We started the meeting with the idea that eventually someone who knew something about ACoA might eventually show up, take over, and start running the meeting for us. We were hoping that would happen. 'Hey, we're running this 12-step meeting inside a distillery.

Someone should probably come and stop us!' I had those sorts of thoughts. That person never showed up, and that meeting is still running over four years later. The distillery has since closed, but the meeting is still running. So the meeting kept going, and then people started claiming that the meeting itself had saved their lives from suicidal ideation and other Complex-PTS-related issues.

"In showing up to the meetings with other people who were struggling with the same issues, we all learned to be authentic and vulnerable together. We did it as a group. Then I started leading other people through the work. Others who attended the meeting went off to start their own meeting. Everyone in and around the meeting started to heal. You know what that means, my little potted friend?"

Franco: "What?"

Me: "That means I suddenly have value! When people tell you that your work has saved their lives, suddenly, one has value. I found my sense of purpose and value in service to others and being a positive contributing part of something much larger than myself. That wasn't a big shift for me. I had a sense of purpose when I was in the military and in law enforcement. My purpose was, 'I'm the guy you send in after the bad guys.' That was my purpose. When I broke away from service, I was just sort of drifting through life (drifting toward suicide).

"The lack of community and isolation felt incredibly isolating. I found my community by finding others who were struggling in the same fashion that I was, and by helping them find peace and joy in their lives (while not neglecting my own), I started creating value in myself as a person. You want to know an added extra bonus in finding a sense of value and purpose in oneself?"

Franco: "Absolutely."

Me: "When my sense of value and purpose comes from within and not in the eyes of others, I no longer have to respond to insults. Insults from others have almost no effect on me. When someone insults me, I might glance inside to see if what they are saying is true or not. Usually, it's not, so I don't have to respond in kind. I find myself not getting into arguments in which I have to defend myself anymore. Here, write this down, Franco."

Franco: "Uh, wait, I don't have a pen. I don't have hands to hold the pen!"

Me: "On your heart then. Write this on your heart, Franco. Anger is the human-expressed form of fear and sadness. Write it down and repeat it until you have it memorized, and it becomes your way of being. It's an important thing to remember, and it's day one, lesson one of Save A Warrior. Knowing this has saved me from engaging in arguments with angry people.

"When someone insults me, my old tendency was to want to be right, valid, and justified and dominate them in the pursuing argument. Those are natural human instincts. 'Whatever you do, plus one, that's what you get back.' The insults would fire back and forth until the tensions rose, sometimes even to the level of physical violence. When I know that anger is the human-expressed form of fear and sadness, when someone hurls an angry insult at me, I just examine myself. I ask myself, 'Is what they are saying possibly true?' If it is not, I just let the angry insult fly by like an arrow that missed its mark. I do not respond by firing back. The way most arguments go in our society is one person defends themself from an insult, lobs one back, and back and forth it goes until it all erupts like a volcano. Not responding to anger with more anger is one of the most challenging things for a human to do. However, when one's sense of value and personal self-worth comes from within themselves, it's not that difficult.

"I was in a meeting and had someone attack me in an angry manner. As the person hurled insults at me, I first knew what they said was not valid. So the arrow didn't land. Then instead of responding in a similar manner, I just watched them and told myself, 'Anger is the human-expressed form of fear and sadness. What I am witnessing is their own fear and sadness based on their own past experiences being aimed at me. Their anger actually has nothing to do with me.' I let the person's rage come all the way out, and when they were finished, the anger just vaporized like a fart and disappeared. After the meeting, witnesses came to me astonished and asked, 'How did you do that? You just sat there as the arrows flew by, and then all of the anger disappeared!' Not responding to hate with hate is one of the most difficult things for a human to do, per Anthony De Mello.

"Per the DeMello Spirituality Center, the three most difficult things for a human to do are not feats of strength or personal achievement. The three hardest things are:
1. Returning love for hate
2. Including the excluded
3. Admitting when we are wrong

"To build a sense of value in oneself, I highly recommend first doing some work on themselves in whatever area of life one needs healing. Alcoholism, drug addiction, gambling, sex addiction, whatever the issue is. Then, once one has a confident sense of healing under their belt, turn around and help someone else get to the level of healing they are at. That's the beauty of a 12-step program. I can immediately turn around and help someone get to the step I just accomplished. If I'm on step 4, someone who has already completed the program is most likely helping me get to step 4, but then I turn around and help someone get to step 1 or 2. In that manner, we are all traveling in the same direction."

Franco: "You immediately have value. You're helping someone else recover."

Me: "Roger that."

Resentment

Me: "He who blames his problems on others extends his own suffering."

Franco: "Did you get that one from Confucius too?"

Me: "No. The Dalai Lama. Confucius might have said something similar. I don't know. I don't even know that the Dalai Lama said that exact same thing. I just happened to be studying him, and the words formed in my head, so I wrote them down in my heart. I found them to be true. I think every major religion and spiritual path I've explored contains some variation of that statement. A central theme that's throughout this book is a saying that I attribute to Confucius, who said, 'He who dwells in the past will be filled with depression. He who dwells in the future will be filled with fear and anxiety. Only he who can dwell in this present moment will ever have peace and tranquility.' The resentment I hold toward others is one of the major things that prevent me from dwelling in the present moment.

"If one studies religious and spiritual paths of healing with an honest, open, and willing perspective, one will notice more similarities than differences. The central characters all tend to agree with each other on their significant points of wisdom. But I only find that which I am looking for. If I look for differences, I will only see differences. If I look for similarities, I will find those instead.

"The resentment I held toward other people and other organizations was a major contributing factor as to why I was having a bad life experience. When I learned to let go of my resentments, my life experience improved immediately."

Franco: "I imagine that is what you're going to talk about now."

Me: "And you would be correct, my little photosynthesizing, light-processing friend. Draw a line in your mind, and make it a timeline. The front tip of the line we will label 'the past.' On the other end, we will label 'the future.' Right in the very middle of that line, put a dot, and we will label that dot 'the present.' The resentments I hold toward others, where would I place those on that timeline?"

Franco: "Well, they're based on my past experiences, so somewhere in the past."

Me: "Exactly. Remember, my brain is all wired for survival. So if I am placing an item on that timeline, that means I have a story or some sort of significance tied to that event. If I'm holding resentment toward someone, that means it's a negative experience, so my amygdala is going to be keeping track of that event, putting it in the 'recently viewed documents' section of my mind, and keeping track of it. That will be pulling my focus off the dot in the center of the timeline and causing me to focus on the past."

Franco: "Where there is depression."

Me: "Yes. All of those dark, bitter emotions that well inside me whenever I consider that event would be my depression. Because it's now in my 'recently viewed documents,' my brain will constantly be drawing my attention to it. Because I am not complete with that event, I am holding on to it as if I am holding on to a marker for a debt. 'Somebody owes me something; I am not complete.' As long as I'm holding on to those resentments, I'm holding on to the trauma surrounding the event as well. The person I'm holding bitterness toward is always going to be occupying my mind, and not in a good way.

"My amygdala, the part of my brain that predicts the future, will constantly be predicting the future because of resentment. It will be plotting out ways to even the debt. I will be dwelling on the past and the future at the same time, experiencing both depression and anxiety. Ironically, as much as I may dislike the person I am holding resentment toward, I'm keeping that relationship alive in my mind for as long as I hold on to the debt because we are not 'complete' in my mind.

"That's what being complete with my past or being complete with someone means. Nobody owes anyone anything. When I am complete, I can let go. When I am not complete, I cannot let go because I am holding on to that debt like it's an IOU. My mind is keeping track of the receipts and who owes me what. Holding onto IOUs is painful and might even be altering my view of that person into always being negative. Until I let go of the debt, I can only see that person in a negative light as someone who owes me something.

"My brain will constantly be scanning the future for others who might screw me over in a similar fashion in the future. I always find exactly what I'm looking for. If I'm constantly looking for people who want to screw me over (because I hold this debt of someone who did it before), I will see a world full of assholes and charlatans. The resentment I'm holding is not only tainting my view of that one person but also contaminating my view of the entire world."

Franco: "Extending my own suffering."

Me: "It's extending my suffering in space, tainting my view of the world, and in time. Here is some logic to consider and relates to how I further extend my own suffering. When I am holding resentment toward someone, the things I am not considering are the fact that they might not give a shit about the debt, might enjoy knowing that I am now suffering in life, or even hold a different version of events inside their thinking in which I owe them."

Franco: "Preposterous!"

Me: "Whatever the case is, they will have no interest in ever getting flat with me on this debt that I think they owe me. I will be extending my own suffering for as long as this occurs."

Franco: "What's the solution?"

Me: "It's very simple. Let go of the debt. Just let go of it. Simply consider letting go of the debt, and I notice peace and tranquility start pouring into my mind and life experience. Suddenly, the sun seems brighter, the air smells cleaner, and little cartoon birds start flying around."

Franco: "You're being cheeky."

Me: "I am. I don't actually see cartoon birds flying around. That might be a legitimate cause for concern. I tell folks, 'I forgive others quickly so that I can get back to enjoying my life as soon as possible.' Consider the best revenge is always living an enjoyable life. One cannot do that if they are carrying a load of resentment. Also, no one ever dies wishing they could hold on to their resentments and more of them longer. Want to take it a step further and get really complete?"

Franco: "Yes."

Me: "I look inward, with integrity, and consider where my resentment is based solely on my judgment of that other person. All humans are seeking happiness and an end to their suffering. When I understand that, then I know that no matter what they're doing that I disapprove of, they do it as an action to end their own suffering. I might disapprove of what they have done, but at least now I understand why they have done it, and I can develop empathy. I am also seeking happiness and an end to my suffering.

"Is my resentment merely due to a differing opinion, preference, or desire? Again, I say that if I learn to hold fewer opinions, I will enjoy my life experience even more. Another good question I ask myself is, 'Am I guilty of the same behavior that I am seeing in them and now judging them for and now holding this resentment against them?' Many times when I judge people, I examine myself and discover I am guilty of the same behavior (I just disguise it better or use different avenues). There is an AA saying that states: 'If you spot it, you got it.' If I can answer yes to any of that, then to really get complete with the situation and let go, I might need their forgiveness for me judging them, making them wrong.

"When I forgive that other person, I release both them and myself from the debt that I am holding. I free two people! Then, when I am no longer viewing the other person through the filter of resentment, I oddly find that I can start liking that person. I noticed that they had good qualities that I liked that I had never noticed before because I was so focused on the resentment aspect of the relationship, viewing them through the filter of that resentment. The possibility exists that once I let go of my resentment, I begin to repair that relationship because I value it. Without the resentment chaining my perspective of life to an event in the past, I dwell in this present moment and enjoy peace in my life."

Franco: "Forgiveness good. Resentment bad."

Me: "Basically."

Honest, Open, Willing

Franco: "What's that mean? Honest, open, willing."

Me: "That's what one has to be to basically grab hold of some wisdom and reinvent themselves using specific spiritual paths, such as the one at Save A Warrior. When I walked into my cohort, I was a bit of a challenge. My way of being was, 'I like to dominate to avoid being dominated, and I'm kind of lazy, so I like to intimidate people. If I can intimidate you, and I see it in your eyes, then I don't even have to dominate you anymore.' I have a story about how I got tricked into being there. I called them to donate money to their cause. SAW sent a representative to the distillery and sort of tricked me into submitting an application."

Franco: "You called to donate money and ended up going through their program instead?"

Me: "Yes, basically. Save A Warrior is the only charity I've ever called to donate money that didn't just hold their hand out and take it from me. They wouldn't take my money until they helped me first. The representative they sent, a fellow by the name of Pat Atkinson, could tell that I was suffering severely from Complex PTS and needed their help."

Franco: "How could he tell?"

Me: "Because he had Complex PTS too, went through their program, and did the work to recover himself. A recovered drug addict can easily spot other drug addicts. An alcoholic can spot other alcoholics. Once one recovers themselves from an issue, they dwell in the realm of 'knowing.' Pat could tell after a brief conversation that I needed help for Complex PTS, fast.

"Another way to spin that whole story is to say some people who loved me wanted to make sure I got the help I needed. Thank God! The program saved my life. But I definitely felt like I got tricked into being there when I got there. As I was about to step through the doorway into my experience, my anxiety was pretty high, so my default way of being was on full display.

"I walked into the room and started eyeballing everyone in there, looking around for the Navy SEAL types, the SWAT guys, and the tactical folks. Essentially I'm 'eye-f*cking' everyone in the room because that's what I do. That's my 'way of being.'"

Franco: "Sounds sketchy."

Me: "Absolutely. I was a sketchy dude who did sketchy stuff. Thank God Adam Carr caught me doing that and told me to 'Stop right there. Are you honest, open, and willing?' I considered the question and chuckled, 'Ha, of course, I am.' Everyone likes to think they're honest, open, and willing. He said, 'No, I mean honest as in, I'm going to stick to the truth, even if I don't like what the truth has to say, I'm going to stick to the truth anyway simply because it's the truth. Do you have it like that?' I thought about it and responded, 'That kind of insinuates that you're going to tell me some stuff I don't want to hear, but I reckon I'll stick to the truth because it's the truth.' He said, 'Good. And are you open to the possibility that the reason my life is appearing the way it does now is 100 percent my responsibility, and you're not blaming all of your life's problems on other people?' I thought about that and said, 'There are some folks out there in the world who owe me a pound of flesh, but I will own what is mine.' He said, 'That's fine. Now, if you're not happy with the way life is appearing to you, are you coachable? Are you willing to consider a new way of seeing things?' I thought about that and responded, 'I'm kind of set in my ways, but I will hear you out and consider new things.' Adam said, 'Outstanding. Have a seat. We're going to start a conversation. You can stop me from talking the moment I say something that you know for certain is a lie.' That last statement made me listen really hard, Franco."

Franco: "Why?"

Me: "Because I was an asshole, and I wanted to be the guy who pointed out all the lies. Except nothing I heard in the pursuing conversation violated my image of God or my internal set of rules of how life works. I heard a bunch of things I had never considered before, and in that realm (the realm of things I didn't know that I didn't know about life), I saw an entirely different way of being available to me in which all of the rules were different.

"The standards by which I measured myself were different. The things I thought were important were suddenly not crucial in the other way of being. The things that I considered trivial and ignored my entire life appeared to make me a wealthy person in this other way of being. This other way of being seemed doable, 'I'm going to try it on for a bit.' When I did, my marriage repaired itself. My family repaired itself. Every relationship I had in life blossomed in this other way of being.

"Being honest, open, and willing saved my life from Complex PTS, and I'm not terminally unique. The vast majority of people who lean into this path of wisdom have their lives transformed. I've since remained honest, open, and willing to a fault, and my life has continued to blossom and become more and more enjoyable to me. What was causing me a lot of misery in life was my stuckness and rigidness. I'm not that way any longer."

Franco: "Schaweet. Anything else?"

Me: "Yes. Another thing that struck me and got my head spinning when I first got there was the cost of the seat. One of the first things they mentioned was how much the seat cost to go through their program."

Franco: "Did you just break out your wallet?"

Me: "No, I immediately got up to leave. I started walking out, and Adam asked, 'Where are you going?' I said, 'I don't have that kind of money, I don't have health insurance, and I'm not looking to acquire any new bills.' He stated, 'Your seat has already been paid for.' I didn't know what to make of that. I looked around the room and asked, 'Are you sure you have the correct

Larry Turner? I'm not really worth anything to anybody.' He replied, 'Please sit down. We have the right Larry, and your seat has been paid for by someone who loves you. Rest assured.'

"That stunned me. I couldn't even conceive of the idea that someone else paid that amount of money for me to sit here and have this experience. It also made me think, *If someone else paid that much money for me to sit here, the least I can do in return is listen to what they have to say.* The fact that someone else paid for me to have the experience definitely caused me to lean into the wisdom more. It was humbling, it saved my life, and that was the first expression of unconditional love I remember ever experiencing.

"It wasn't the last. I see acts of unconditional love (love with no strings attached) constantly at Save A Warrior. It saves lives. Since then, I have been constantly trying to devise ways of raising money to pay for others' seats. When the warrior sits in the seat, they are blindsided by the fact that it's a warrior-led nontransactional experience. Those are the magical ingredients that are reversing the veteran/first-responder suicide epidemic due to Complex PTS.

"Complex PTS is PTS that begins in childhood, compounded by the moral injuries one endures on the battlefield or on the streets as a first responder. The two collapse and morph into Complex PTS. Essentially, the cure is wisdom served with unconditional love, no strings attached."

Franco: "Gotcha. Well, then this ends this book, I take it? What's next? Want to do a sequel? Can it be one with car chases and war stories?"

Me: "Well, I've already got a working title for the next book."

Franco: "Ooh! What's it called?"

Me: "*Franco, the Succulent Lands on the Neighbor's Roof.*"

Franco: "That...but that doesn't make any sense."

Me: "It will after you get into this potato cannon."

Franco: "Hey!"

Me: "I'm kidding! I'm probably just going to take a break for a bit, catch up on some reading. I've got a lot of books on my reading list. We'll pick it up again soon. I've got lots more I want to talk to you about."

Franco: "Peace!"

Boundaries—
Emotional Sobriety

Franco: "I heard you discussing with someone that they couldn't achieve emotional sobriety until they had physical sobriety. What exactly is emotional sobriety, and why do I need to be physically sober to get it?"

Me: "Well, it almost takes a perspective from a spiritual point of view to fully wrap my human brain around it all, and for that, I need physical sobriety to comprehend. My internal emotions are my spirit's nerve endings. I cannot numb my spirit's nerve endings and notice why they are responding the way they do at the same time. It's self-defeating.

"That and what I am about to say requires a sober mind to comprehend. If my emotions are out of whack and I'm on what one would describe as an emotional roller coaster, what I possibly have are errors in the internal logic programming of my mind's thinking processes. That requires distinctions to correct. Epiphanies. Epiphanies and distinctions are a lot easier to come by with a sober mind."

Franco: "A sober mind is required for epiphanies. Epiphanies are required to unravel the human experience."

Me: "That's been my experience. I didn't start having mental and spiritual epiphanies until I gained physical sobriety. Until then, life was a mess. I had my personal emotions and problems confused with other people's. My problems in life are my problems in life. Your problems are your problems. Until I understood the boundaries that divided them, I had a habit of assuming responsibility for your problems. Your problems became my problems."

Franco: "That's a whole lot of problems!"

Me: "I'm not terminally unique, my little sun worshipper. Many people have an overdeveloped sense of personal responsibility. That is yet another side effect of being raised in a dysfunctional family environment. As children, we think it's our responsibility to keep the peace in the house and that it's typically our fault if there isn't any. We begin confusing the boundaries of my problems and your problems before we even understand that we're doing it. By the time we become adults, we have the perspective that 'It's always been that way.' We get used to it. We get used to dysfunction, it becomes our 'normal.' In fact, all of the misery and suffering becomes normal also. Humans can get addicted to the suffering associated with shame. In that manner, misery becomes as comfortable as an old pair of tennis shoes."

Franco: "That's a frightening way to exist."

Me: "Many people are doing it, Franco. My inner feelings and emotions are also my personal responsibility. Yours are yours. That is another boundary that tends to get blurry by an unsober person. My personal feelings and emotions are the nerve endings of my spirit, essentially. My feelings and emotions are being experienced inside of my meat puppet, so they are exclusively my responsibility. Not yours.

"When I understand this boundary, you won't have the ability to 'piss me off' anymore. You really never have, and what I am gaining is an awareness of that fact. An emotionally sober and responsible person realizes they are simply choosing to be pissed off and need to understand why they are allowing themselves to be in that mental state. So when negative emotions such as sadness, anxiety, or anger start to emerge, what a physically unsober person will be tempted to do is to spiritually bypass (numb/place the life experience on pause) those negative feelings and emotions."

Franco: "That's why they call it 'numbing.'"

Me: "Absolutely. I'm often first invalidating the internal feelings (not taking responsibility for them) and then numbing them to make them more bearable. Pretend that whatever it is that's causing the negative feelings is a splinter in my hand. The splinter hurts going in and continues to cause pain until I deal with it and actually take the splinter out.

"I can distract myself from the splinter by staying busy. I used to tell people I was 'good with the world, as long as it was going a thousand miles per hour. It's when it slows down, and I'm alone with my thoughts, that I have problems.' That's sort of like me working overtime every chance I get so that I'm not alone with my thoughts."

Franco: "If you're focusing on work, you're not focusing on the splinter!"

Me: "I'm distracting myself from the splinter by staying busy at work. As soon as I'm not at work, however, I'm reminded that the splinter is still in my hand, and suddenly it hurts again. I can numb the area that the splinter is in with drugs and alcohol, and that will provide me with temporary relief. Soon, however, the numbness wears off, and the splinter hurts again.

"The splinter will continue to hurt, possibly getting worse and getting infected, until I first acknowledge that the splinter is there, take responsibility for it, and pull the splinter out. Then the wound around the splinter heals. Once I have physical sobriety and stop numbing the splinters, then I can take a good look at them and pull them out. That's emotional sobriety."

Franco: "So, in this analogy, the emotions are splinters?"

Me: "No. The pain I am feeling internally due to the splinter are my emotions. The splinters are the thing that's causing the physical pain, or rather negative internal emotions. When I stop numbing my feelings/emotions and instead start to understand them, I can get to the root of the pain (take out the splinters).

"The first step is I have to feel my feelings and take responsibility for them. I quit invalidating, denying, and numbing them.

When I blame my internal feelings and emotions on other people or other things, I extend my own suffering."

Franco: "It's almost like I create a trap and then step into my own trap by doing that."

Me: "Let's take anger, for instance. That is a common one that I often hear. 'So and so has pissed me off!' The statement itself is untrue. In order for the other person to be able to cause negative emotional feelings inside me, their spirit would have to be with me, inside my meat puppet, with their hands on the controls of my internal feelings. My anger is felt inside of myself by me. You do not have the power to control my internal emotions. To think you have the power to piss me off would be an error in logic. If I give you the power to upset me, I have become your emotional slave. In this manner, I am being co-dependent (all driven by abandonment terror). A codependent person places control of their internal emotional state (happiness/sadness/joy/anger) into the care of another person. I have to grant you full control over my internal emotional state in order to allow you to do that."

Franco: "Let's pretend a friend of mine does that..."

Me: "Are you talking about yourself?"

Franco: "Maybe. It doesn't matter. Let's say I know someone who does that."

Me: "Is his name Franco? Is he green in color and perhaps lives in a pot on my bookshelf?"

Franco: "It doesn't matter who! Damn it, you're pissing me off! Well, okay, yes, it is me. What's the alternative?"

Me: "The alternative is to take responsibility for one's own internal emotions. It's just a distinction that I create inside my mind. These are my emotions inside of me, and those are yours inside yourself. Recognize the boundary between them. I cannot control your emotions inside of you, and you cannot control mine inside of me."

Franco: "And then I'll never get angry again?"

Me: "Incorrect, my little water hoarder. I will still get upset occasionally. There are hills and valleys in life. Good things are always going to happen, and bad things are always going to happen. The key to a peaceful life is to let it all flow like water and never get too attached to anything. I remind myself that whether it's a good experience or bad: 'This too shall pass.'

"I've studied the Tao, and they remind me that everything in life has an equal opposite. The yin and the yang. There could never be a 'here' without an 'over there.' There couldn't possibly be a black without a white to contrast with. There cannot be an up without a down, and I would never know that I dislike something unless I experienced something in contrast what I like.

"In life, good things and bad things are going to be coming and going into my life. If I don't allow myself to get attached to either good or bad and just accept life as it happens, I become the 'observer' of life, and life just flows along. Even if I am experiencing a perfect period of my life, I know that eventually, something will happen out here in the game, and I won't like it. When that happens, the first step for me is to notice that I am getting upset. I don't like being upset, so I try to notice that I'm becoming upset as quickly as possible. Someone else might even point it out before I notice. 'Larry, you seem upset.' Rather than deny that I am upset, stuff the feelings away internally, and defend myself, I reflect inward and evaluate myself to see if they are correct and, if so, determine why I am upset. I don't invalidate my feelings and emotions. Rather, I notice them and take responsibility for them. They are being experienced by my spirit, inside of me, so I try to notice them as quickly as possible.

"Internally, I talk to myself. I know that all anger is a human-expressed form of fear and sadness. So I ask myself, 'What am I possibly sad or fearful of now?' I've noticed some common denominators from examining my own emotional states. If someone hurls an insult at me and I begin to get angry, it is usually due to one of two things."

Franco: "Only one of two things?"

Me: "For the most part. Either I secretly fear that what they are saying about me is true, and I fear now being exposed, or I want something from that person (usually their acceptance). The insult they've cast toward me is indicative that they now regard me with shame and judgment. Thus, I'm not going to get what I want, which is their approving attitude toward me."

Franco: "If someone insults you, either what they're saying is true, or you want something from them and are now not going to get it?"

Me: "Usually not either/or, more like a combination of both. See, the only way the arrow they've hurled at me in the form of an insult can hit its mark and cause the negative emotional pain response being felt inside me is if one of those two things happens to be correct. The solution for me has been to stop defending myself from insults. I mean, why bother?"

Franco: "When I stop defending myself, I stop inviting attacks. And often, when I am mad and judging someone, if I examine myself with humility, I will find I am typically guilty of the same behavior. I just think I'm better at masking it."

Me: "Where did you learn that?"

Franco: "You have me sitting on this bookshelf. It's boring in here when you're gone. I read a lot."

Me: "I cannot control what other people think about me, and I only spend energy on things I can control. Your thoughts and opinions about me are not one of those things."

Franco: "Gnarly."

Me: "If I hold my sense of personal value within myself by living a purposeful life, then I no longer find my value in the eyes of other people. Because my sense of value comes from myself, I no longer respond to shaming attacks from others. Emotional sobriety makes those attacks meaningless. I cease wanting things from other people. When I stop wanting things from other people, their ability to harm me with insults vaporizes. But wait! There's more!"

Franco: "As an extra special bonus gift?"

Me: "Our operators are standing by. If you act now, in addition to emotional sobriety for oneself, we are all spirits having a human experience, and if my anger is fear and sadness being expressed by myself, then I know that to be true of the person insulting me also.

"With enough practice, I can develop these neural pathways so that I have these thought patterns very quickly. These are distinctions that I build into my internal logic programming, and soon they happen quite quickly, changing the way I respond to events happening in the world. As soon as someone insults me, I begin developing compassion for them."

Franco: "When someone spouts off angrily toward you, instead of defending yourself, you have compassion for them? Isn't that a weakness? I thought you were a warrior!"

Me: "That's the path of confidence, not weakness. Responding to anger with more anger is actually lazy. Responding to anger with love and kindness is one of the most challenging and difficult things for a human to do, per Anthony De Mello. So it actually demonstrates courage and spiritual strength to do so. It may be regarded as a weakness by those following the ruler of the physical world. That's a tough world out there. I don't follow those rules. There's no need to. My life actually works, and I enjoy life."

Franco: "Boosh! Do you want to be right or be happy? You can choose only one!"

Me: "I'm glad you're paying attention! No one who has chosen happiness has ever regretted their choice. If I know my feelings of internal anger are based on my own fear or sadness, the same is true for them. As they are insulting me, what I am witnessing is their own fear and sadness being expressed at me. The fear and sadness they have is based upon their own past experiences and thus have nothing to do with me. I want nothing from them, so my sense of personal value is not threatened. Once I realize all that, their insult flies past me like an arrow that has missed its mark."

Franco: "Level up on agility!"

Me: "When I don't return their anger with my own anger (defending invites more attack), their anger usually vanishes quite quickly. No one likes wasting arrows."

Franco: "A warrior would know."

Me: "That's some spiritual kung fu! Now, let's back up. Say someone insults me, and upon examining myself, I find that the reason I am experiencing anger internally is that I feel what they are saying is true. Now I have some work to do.

"Instead of defending myself from the insult, I take the perspective that what they are saying is correct. What they have done is expose a flaw in my character that I perhaps was unaware of. Now, they have given me a gift! They have exposed a weakness in my armor! With this perspective, I see they are attacking me with gifts."

Franco: "Whatever doesn't kill me makes me stronger."

Me: "I concur."

Franco: "So, you just woke up one day and had all this, or you read a book, or what?"

Me: "Do you know how to get to Broadway, Franco?"

Franco: "No, how?"

Me: "Practice! Lots and lots of practice."

Franco: "Ha!"

Me: "I do read a lot, but I also go to lots of meetings. I go to 12-step meetings where I meet other people doing this work on themselves. I learn from them. I do the work on myself and then lead others through the work. I hold myself accountable to other safe people who are doing the work on themselves.

"When I'm having a bad day, I don't dwell alone in my suffering and pretend everything is okay. As soon as I notice that I'm experiencing negative emotions, I acknowledge those emotions and then try to sort out why they're happening. I might need to pick up that thousand-pound telephone and call someone else for help."

Franco: "Phones are that heavy? I never held one so I didn't know. Man, you must be like Thor. You're on it all the time."

Me: "No, it just seems like it's a thousand pounds sometimes, particularly when I have to admit that I'm struggling. In the mindset I've held for most of my life, admitting that I am struggling was regarded as weakness, thus very difficult to do."

Franco: "If you want to go fast, go alone. If you want to go far, go together."

Me: "Roger that! I prefer internal feelings of peace. So when I notice that I'm getting upset about something or at someone, if I can't sort it out on my own and return to peace quickly, I'll phone a friend. When they answer, I say, 'I am not calling to spread gossip nor am I looking for someone to commiserate with. Do not repeat anything I am about to say to you. I am looking for someone to hear me out and offer an alternate perspective on things. Are you open?'

"When they say, 'I'm open. Hit me!' then I will lay out that which I am struggling with. Most often, my friends will offer me a fresh perspective, which, if I embrace it, dissipates my anger. Sometimes they cannot offer that perspective and just say, 'I'm sorry to hear that. I cannot offer an alternative perspective. That is truly fucked up.' Even in that case, I no longer suffer alone. The vile anger is now out of me, and my friend has eased the burden of it by simply hearing me out. The key is to never suffer life alone."

Franco: "The path of joy is in connection. The path of suffering is in isolation."

Me: "Outstanding, Franco! Did you just come up with that?"

Franco: "No, that was the Dalai Lama and Desmond Tutu in *The Book of Joy*."

Me: "Great book! Well, I have to go, so I will see you later. I have STDs."

Franco: "Uh, you have STDs?"

Me: "Yep! I have a ton of STDs! Shit to do."

Franco: "Oh! Thank God!"

Me: "Yeah, my wife hates when I say that. She says, 'That makes people think I must have STDs too!' I tell her, 'You do! You're as busy as a bee! When I tell people I have STDs, they kind of just look at me funny and slowly back away, allowing me to get my STDs done."

Franco: "She rolls her eyes at you a lot, doesn't she?"

Me: "Her eye muscles look like they were raised in a gym."

Vulnerability— Non-shareable Problems

Franco: "I saw you spraying the weeds outside. Please wash your hands before you touch me."

Me: "I wasn't planning on physically touching you, Franco. When was the last time I've actually touched you? I'll give you a hint; it rhymes with 'never.' I talk to you, but I never touch you. That seems like an unreasonable fear that you possess. Why is that?"

Franco: "Why is that? Because I believe the stuff you are spraying out there is poison, at least to plants. I am a plant. Aren't you afraid of poison?"

Me: "Meh. Maybe when I was a kid. That and quick sand. I thought that was going to a much bigger problem in life. Eating military MREs broke me of fear of poison. I remember eating those and thinking, *This meal was prepared for me by the lowest bidder on a government contract.* I was either going to eat it or go hungry. Eventually, I ate one and survived. After that, I learned to eat pretty much anything."

Franco: "Were there any bad side effects?"

Me: "Well, I probably didn't shit for a week afterward, but other than that, no."

Franco: "Ha! That ended your fear of poison."

Me: "I mean, I can still get food poisoning. I am human. My meat puppet can still get ill. However, what is more concerning to me now is that which would poison my spirit. That's what I have to be on guard for."

Franco: "What is poison to the human spirit?"

Me: "Shame. Shame will wreak havoc on my spirit and my life experience. Shame is the major driving force behind suicide. That is why pills typically only offer limited relief. One is attempting to apply a physical solution to a spiritual problem. The good news is I always carry the antidote."

Franco: "What is the antidote for shame?"

Me: "Vulnerability. Shame will drive a person to suicide. The antidote to shame is the expression of vulnerability with another human. The shame vaporizes in the connections that develop between one spirit to another. What's difficult for most humans is that the antidote sometimes looks scarier than the poison. Vulnerability looks like a giant horse pill to some

and appears challenging to swallow. The depth of my relationship with others is measured in vulnerability and authenticity.

"Most relationships out there in the physical world are very
shallow, and I don't notice that. They're based on 'looking
good.' Out there, I'm concerned with looking good to avoid
looking bad. Them's the rules out there. They're brutal."

Franco: "Ah, that's why I always hear you asking people if they
have non-shareable problems! I wasn't sure what a non-shareable problem was. I get it. It's shame!"

Me: "Well, it's a piece of shame about myself that I hide because I don't want others to know about it. A non-shareable
problem is something I don't want you to figure out about me.
I think that once you figure this out about me, you'll always be
looking at me sideways, there'll probably be questions I don't
want to answer, and I might get kicked off the team. A non-
shareable problem limits the depth of a relationship I can have
with another human spirit, thus limits the depth of my connections with others and limits my ability to heal my spirit. The
human spirit is designed for two things, Franco. It is designed
for struggle."

Franco: "The world is full of struggle."

Me: "That's what life is, a series of problems. Struggle. The
other thing the human spirit is designed for is connection with
others. It is in the depth of our connections with one another
that the burden of our struggles is lifted. Non-shareable problems keep those connections with others shallow, leaving me
to struggle all by myself."

Franco: "So shame and non-shareable problems are the same things?"

Me: "For the most part. Tomayto, tomahto."

Franco: "So, when someone answers you saying, 'No...'"

Me: "It's very rare that someone tells me that they have no non-shareable problems after I go through some examples, but on occasion, one denies having them. When they do that, they're telling me that they have no shame about themselves. They're addicted to 'looking good.' I remind them that no one comes to us because they've won the lottery and that this is not a place to come and 'look good' while one is healing."

Franco: "Healing is ugly."

Me: "There will be tears when one is faced with the source of own shame, but then there is the relief that comes on the other side that makes the fear of shame suddenly insignificant. Often the sense of relief is so intense that the person experiencing it immediately starts looking for more shame to offload with others. They suddenly realize that fear of shame is an illusion."

Franco: "As if fear of shame is greater than the shame itself. I saw a news story about a person who was constantly on the run from the law, expressing great relief when they were finally caught. It seemed like an odd thing to me, that getting caught actually provided freedom to them. That seems like the same thing."

Me: "It is! Suddenly, I am free of the burden from that which is haunting me. One has to be willing to look bad to get in the other side of their shame. When one denies having non-shareable problems, automatically a red flag goes up for me in my mind. They're telling me that they have done nothing in life that they hold any sort of shame about. Essentially, I am to assume they are like Jesus or something. They're telling me they're still on the run, and they're not interested in stopping.

"My next question is, 'Then why are you coming to us, a suicide detox facility? Our way out is straight through the shame, which you deny having any of.' Shame is the main cause of suicide. By denying that they have shame, they're telling me that they're not interested in the antidote, which is vulnerability and authenticity with others."

Franco: "What are the examples of the non-shareable problems you give?"

Me: "One night, in a convoy on deployment, I think I might have run over a child. They might be dead, I have no idea. Or, I killed someone on purpose, and now I question that entire scenario. I was raped. I'm gay, or I am bisexual, and no one knows. I'm addicted to alcohol, drugs, gambling, pornography, or whatever. I was molested by a relative, a neighbor, a teacher, clergy, or whomever. I cheated on my spouse. I stole something. I believe I am a fraud. The person I am presenting to the world is in contrast to what is going on for me internally. I hit my spouse. My spouse hits me. My children are terrified. I believe my actions have led to the death of another."

Franco: "You hit them with that?"

Me: "Yes. Those are the examples I often give, and I remind them that these might seem like extreme examples, and it is not an all-inclusive list, just a few examples that I would not be interested in engaging in with my buddies in the back of the raid van. If they cannot admit that they possess non-shareable problems of some variety, then there is little use in them coming here because that's what we will be chatting about.

"A lot of people think they're struggling with depression and anxiety in life due to their experiences on the battlefield or the streets. That's not what's driving the depression, anxiety, and suicidal thoughts. What's driving the suicidal thoughts are the feelings of isolation, thinking one is terminally unique. That is caused by a learned way of being, the habit of hiding shame learned from being raised in the cult of culture.

"Combine that with an inability to mourn their grief due to a belief that expressing true emotion is a 'sign of weakness,' it's a suicide-cocktail. Talk about poison, there you go! When I ask someone how they're struggling in life right now, sometimes they hit me with a long war story of something that happened long ago in the past. I will listen for a bit and eventually interrupt them, asking them if they're coachable. When they respond, 'Yes,' I tell them I'm sorry to hear that they've experienced such a traumatic event, but then point out that they have not answered my question. The question was, 'How are you struggling in life right now? See if you can answer that question without telling me of something that happened in the past.' Usually, there's a pause as they consider if they should be offended by my interruption of their story or not, then they realize they have not begun to answer my question honestly.

"Many people have significance of meaning surrounding their stories of trauma. They're used to engaging in transactional-type relationships in which one is doing things in order to solicit a response. I tell you this story 'in order to' solicit sympathy out of you, so I can 'get what I want.' When I stop them and ask the same question more directly, that forces them to consider themselves more honestly, and usually tears follow. They might have a breakdown, which is fine. Breaking down is fine, because intense relief always follows. When one has incredibly vulnerable conversations with others and come off of hidden shame (non-shareable problems), the shallowness of other relationships previously held suddenly becomes obvious.

"The relationships in which I can be authentic and vulnerable become the valuable ones. The shallow relationships that merely exist on the standard of 'looking good' are a dime a dozen. To make a relationship valuable, I become more vulnerable. Typically vulnerability is contagious. As soon as I become more vulnerable, the other person does also."

Franco: "Like kindness, vulnerability is contagious."

Me: "Indeed. Most people are starving for vulnerability and authenticity in their relationships; they just aren't willing to take the first step, and that's understandable. It's a harsh world out there. Most of the relationships out there are based on the code: 'You don't call me on my bullshit, and I won't call you on yours.' That is the level of depth in them. When I become honest with another person about my perceived failings in life, and take ownership of them, that is demonstrating authenticity and vulnerability with them. When that happens, the connection gets deeper. Spirits heal one another on that level.

But it takes courage to get there. One person has to take the first step, and then it becomes a game I like to call 'How honest can you get?' When one can get very honest with someone else, the shame goes away."

Franco: "Shame is poison to the human spirit. Shame is what drive's depression, anxiety, and the main cause of suicide."

Me: "You're repeating what I already said."

Franco: "It's worth repeating."

Me: "I am not being critical; it's just an observation. Shame is the poison that remains in my spirit until I can get vulnerable and authentic about it with another human."

Franco: "In sharing the shame, it vaporizes."

Me: "Yes, but then to *really* get complete with it, I may need to make amends for whatever harm I may have caused, or stop whatever behavior it was that I was engaged in that generated the shame, or there will just be more."

Franco: "I understand. The antidote to shame is vulnerability. Fear of shame is what prevents many people from taking the antidote. They think being authentic about it will lead to more shame. They think they will be shamed, for being vulnerable about their shame."

Me: "It's as if I were talking through you, Franco. And understand, their fear of becoming shamed by becoming vulnerable is a legitimate concern. If one becomes vulnerable with an asshole, they might be shamed, but that's a problem that resolves itself."

Franco: "It self-corrects?"

Me: "It does! All I have to do is take the first step and start being vulnerable, and those people out there in the world will sort themselves out. Those who can't handle vulnerability will start distancing themselves and tossing shame like distraction flares as they leave. That's fine. They might be thinking, *Shoot! This person is going to expect me to be vulnerable about my own shame now! I'm not ready for that. I'm still on the run!* I just let them go with no judgment. They're just not ready for that level of human interaction. 'But by the grace of God go I.'

"Those who can handle that depth of connection will draw themselves closer, attracted by my authenticity. And now my life will get better. I will have higher quality people in my life, thus my life experience will improve. It's a problem that fixes itself. My getting well is not in everyone's best interests. Those who have truly my six and best interests in mind will make themselves known to me. Those who don't will show themselves to the door."

Franco: "A problem that resolves itself!"

Me: "You're repeating me again, just an observation. My life experience improves. I can assume others will probably talk about me behind my back. Again, what other people think about me is none of my business, and I can just assume they're thinking horrible things. They usually are not.

"When one is struggling with shame, I think people are talking about me harshly and casting judgment. That's just what my ego thinks. In reality, people are not thinking about me as much as I think they are, usually never at all."

Franco: "Hey! I have a non-shareable problem I need to get rid of."

Me: "Well, I'm open. Hit me with it."

Franco: "There's a filthy-looking weed out there by the septic tank lid. She might be poison ivy, I'm not certain. I just know that sometimes I catch myself staring at her, and my roots start to tingle a bit."

Me: "Ah, I see. Would you like me to introduce you to her? I could go out and get her, bring her in here with us. Want me to put her next to your pot?"

Franco: "No! Aw, heck no! I have no idea what kind of spores she's carrying. She looks like she's covered in some sort of oil. I don't know what that is, but I don't need any of it on me, I can tell you that."

Me: "Ha! Very well, thank you for sharing. Tell you what, I'll move you over to this window and you can stare out at the apple trees for a while. That might be more wholesome?"

Franco: "Yes, thank you. Hey, you said vulnerability was contagious. Don't you have any non-shareables for me?"

Me: "Ah, yes, of course. Let me think...I've got one."

Franco: "Hit me, I'm open!"

Me: "Sometimes I procrastinate on getting things done."

Franco: "That's it? Are you kidding me? I come off my fantasies about the filthy weed, and that's what you serve back? You procrastinate?"

Me: "Lower your expectations, and you will experience less disappointment in life. Do you know what expectations are, Franco?"

Franco: "Yes, expectations are resentments under development. *Sigh*... Go ahead and just set me by the apple trees, and thank you."

Mourning and Grieving

Me: "I used to have it that if I was not suffering enough on particular anniversaries or depressed enough, I was somehow dishonoring the friends who I lost on those specific dates. I would meet up with others who were also dwelling on the events surrounding the tragedy, and the depression would steadily build throughout the day. By mid-afternoon, I would start numbing, usually by drinking a crazy amount of alcohol. That was how life was.

"Thank God for Save A Warrior for bringing clarity of mind. There were severe errors in my logic for doing things that way that I ignored. One of the errors in logic was the fact that my friends who have passed loved me. For sure, I know they did. They traded their life in defense of mine. If they were still around, they would want me to enjoy what life I had left as thoroughly as possible, even on the anniversaries of their deaths."

Franco: "That's the truth, Ruth!"

Me: "I am eternally grateful to the good people (warriors) who had traveled this path before me and showed me the way to properly mourn my losses and process my past trauma. I am now able to honor my friends now by living a rich, full life, paying my life forward (by practicing good self-care, thus being able to contribute to the wellness of others around me), and being the best example of a human who I can scrape together each day. I use the wisdom gained in the journey of my own healing to assist others who are struggling in a similar fashion. Now, instead of the traumatic event simply residing in my memory as a point of constant depression, my recovery is a tool to connect with and assist in the recovery of others. In that manner, once properly processed, the trauma's value is when used as a device to assist others in their recovery. That is where the term 'wounded healers' stems from.

"In order to be processed, trauma has to be shared with someone who has EARNED the right to hear it and grieved. In that manner, it lessens the pain of the event that resides within the memory of my own life experience. Healing doesn't come simply in the telling of old war stories, however. That is why one can often find depressed people sitting around in bars, recounting old war stories with one another and numbing at the same time. One has to mourn and grieve their losses in the company of other safe people. That is how trauma leaves the human body."

Franco: "Through tears."

Me: "Correctamundo. We are trained as children that 'big boys don't cry,' and in the warrior communities, those who do so are often regarded with shame or as weak. Without expressing the trauma of the events through tears (which is how humans express grief), the trauma has nowhere to go. It is therefore stored and hidden away inside the brain's data banks as an unprocessed 'painful memory.' Left unprocessed, the amygdala will constantly refer to it, thus causing panic attacks, hypervigilance, high blood pressure, heart attacks, and general irritability."

Franco: "Is that all?"

Me: "No. I could fill a book with the horrible mental/physical/spiritual side effects of unprocessed trauma, like a television commercial for the latest new drugs. 'May cause loose bowel movements and the inability to control them.'"

Franco: "Oh! Sign me up for that!"

Me: "God, you're weird. That's probably why they hid you so far back on that shelf in the nursery. I thought you were just in the scratch-and-dent section. Sometimes these memories can be buried so deep they are somewhat forgotten, only re-emerging when the person is mentally and spiritually ready to process the event. A question was asked of me: 'Are there any sayings that you repeat to yourself throughout the day?'

"Here is one that I say often and have already written about. I learned it when I was a small child, and it has been written in my heart ever since, although I didn't fully understand what it meant until I went to SAW. It's from Confucius: 'He who dwells in the past WILL be filled with depression. He who dwells in the future WILL be filled with fear and anxiety. Only he who can reside in this present moment will ever have peace and tranquility.'

"When I focus on my past, I tend to focus on my losses (people and things who aren't here anymore) or shame myself over my own behavior (I should have done that, shouldn't have done that, probably could have done that better). When I focus on the future, I will waste my energy as my mind makes predictions that will never come to pass (usually of the 'worst-case scenario' variety, since my brain is wired for survival).

"I process my losses, grieving, and mourning when needed, and in doing so, the pain and the sting of the events that I have woven into the meaning surrounding it are stripped away. After which, I will find myself less often triggered by events happening in the current moment (where there is peace)."

Franco: "Is that why flashbacks and recurring nightmares happen?"

Me: "Well, I'm no rocket surgeon or brain scientist, Franco, but I did sleep in a Holiday Inn Express last night. The flashbacks and nightmares are caused by the amygdala, the CPU of my brain, which references the unprocessed traumatic items stored in my memory banks that still have painful meanings associated with them.

"The traumatic pain is in the meaning I have attached to an event, not in the facts of what happened. When I separate the two, the memory now dwells as 'something that happened,' which is now significantly less painful once mourned. It will still cause sadness if I dwell on the event."

Franco: "What is the fix for that?"

Me: "Just don't dwell. I can glance at my past but never stare. By mourning and grieving in the company of safe people, I am stripping that pain of the memory away, so the amygdala will have less to reference in the future.

"Without it being referenced as frequently in the past, the amygdala will have less to worry about when it is predicting the future (which I also have to catch myself doing and stop). Based upon what my own eyes have shown me, people tend to struggle less with depression and anxiety after processing their losses and traumatic incidents of their pasts in such a manner."

Franco: "Roger that."

Surrender—Care of God

Me: "Pretend it's a game, take your time, and play like your life depends upon it."

Franco: "What's that?"

Me: "Just something that was written on a piece of paper that I noticed when I started my journey of recovery. It really struck me at the time, it still does, really, and that's just how I approach life and the universe now."

Franco: "You pretend it's a game?"

Me: "Absolutely. And I take my time. And I play like my life depends upon it. What are games supposed to be, Franco?"

Franco: "I don't understand the question. Games are supposed to be..."

Me: "Fun, Franco! Games are supposed to be fun. If games aren't fun, people quit playing them. I wasn't having any fun in my life when I came to Save A Warrior, a suicidal-ideation Complex-PTS detox facility. I wanted to quit playing the game. So when I saw that just as the experience began ('Pretend it's a game, take your time, and play like your life depends upon it'), I thought, *This is apparently how these people want me to approach this experience.* Having that sort of mentality of 'This is just a game' allowed me to transform my life during the program, and I had a spiritual awakening of the educational variety.

"And then, when I left, no one told me to stop doing that, so I just continued with the idea that I was playing a game out there in 'the world.' I started taking my time, and I started playing like my life depended upon it. The spiritual awakening caused me to view all of life differently, in a more fun way.

"I pretend it's a game, and I quit taking life so seriously. I take my time. I always seemed to be in a massive rush before the experience because I was *sooo important.* I was addicted to my own significance as the rescuer of everyone's problems. We're all gonna die, Franco. Tomorrow is never promised to anyone. There's no need to rush the life experience. I learned to slow everything down and start enjoying things a bit more.

"Then I learned to play as my life depended upon it. I realized I was at a suicidal ideation detox facility. So, when people who seemed to actually be enjoying their lives started telling me what the 'rules of life' were that they were playing by, I listened. They told me to readjust my priorities in life and put my recovery at the top of the list. So I did that, and when I did, a fantastic thing happened."

Franco: "What happened?"

Me: "I started having fun. When my views of life and the universe shifted, I thought, *The rules of this game are actually a whole lot more fun than the rules I made up on my own when I was growing up.* See, we're all doing that, Franco."

Franco: "Doing what?"

Me: "We humans are born into this life with no instructions on how to 'play the game.' So we simply make the rules up as we go. We try to figure out what's important out there, but we don't really have the rule sheet for the game. What's really interesting is that what we think is essential typically shifts dramatically as we play the game.

"When we are children and adolescents, what's really important is fitting in with others. We think popularity is the most essential thing, so we put all of our eggs into that basket. We fear shame and begin hiding it so that we don't get outcast from the others playing the game.

"As we get a little older and get into our careers, what's important is the accumulation of stuff. We think acquiring money and stuff is the key to winning the game. We start trading all of our time for money so that we can get more stuff.

"As we get older still and notice that there's more sand in the bottom than the top of the hourglass regulating the game, it suddenly dawns on us that the time we were trading for money was more valuable than the money. The only thing we accumulated by chasing wealth was regret, but that doesn't dawn on us until the end of the game."

Franco: "Why is that?"

Me: "Because God has a sense of humor."

Franco: "Ha! Wait. That's not funny."

Me: "That's all right, my agave. Just as soon as I figured out what the actual rules were, I started having a lot more fun in the game of life immediately."

Franco: "What's the key to finding fun in the game?"

Me: "What works for me is surrender."

Franco: "Surrender? I thought you weren't the type to surrender anything. You are more of a street fighter. What part of life are you talking about surrendering?"

Me: "All of it, every bit of it."

Franco: "Surrender it to whom?"

Me: "My higher power, God. I used to like to think I had surrendered my life to God. I thought I did at one point when I was a kid and first heard about Him, but I wasn't 100 percent sure He knew who I was or maybe He had possibly forgotten about me or something.

"Way back in the very beginning of my life experience, before my ego turned itself on, life was fun. Everything was fresh, and the universe was full of wonder. Each day was a new experience as I explored the world around me (adding meaning to everything/'naming the animals'). It was as if God and I were playing a video game, and it was fun.

"Then my ego came online, and it was as if God got up, handed me the controller for a moment to go to the bathroom or something, and when He came back, I was still sitting in His seat. So He didn't disturb me. He just sat back and watched me pretend to play Him for a while. What father wouldn't want to watch their kids impersonate them? He watched me start calling the shots out there in the game.

"It's like He watched me choose the career path of warrior and thought, *The path of honor, interesting! Let's see how this all pans out!* He just kept standing back, watching. It got really scary and really crazy out there! I did a lot of crazy stuff! I got hurt a few times but always dusted myself off and got back into the game. He just kept watching. He basically watched me steer my meat puppet to a dead end, watched as I investigated and contemplated suicide to get out of the game, and that's when He cleared His throat and asked for the controller back. I handed the controls back, and immediately, a series of incidents happened (I call them miracles). I was suddenly made spiritually aware of myself. The first thing I noticed when I became spiritually aware was that I was sitting in God's seat. I gave Him His seat back and started watching Him play.

"As soon as I surrendered control of my life to God, the experience of life immediately improved for me. Life went from completely sucking to feeling completely blessed just as soon as I did. The first thing He did was turn the meat puppet around and walk it away from the cliff of suicide that I was looking at. He glanced down at the 'rule sheet of life' that I had scribbled down and asked me to read what I had written down."

Franco: "What did He think of your rules?"

Me: "Well, He didn't like them. I had a bunch of 'exceptions' written down."

Franco: "Exceptions?"

Me: "Yeah, like, 'God can be in charge, except when bullets are involved.'"

Franco: "Ha! He didn't like that exception?"

Me: "Not one bit. And, 'God can be in charge, except when I'm at work because somebody's gotta keep the bad guy's scared, and apparently, You suck at it because I have a job!'"

Franco: "Hahaha! You had that written down?"

Me: "Yeah... Hey, I was young. He really frowned at that one but forgave me. He pointed out that the way I had my life organized, I placed myself in charge while I was at work, and when I wasn't at work, I was 'spiritually bypassing' (placing the game on pause), so God had no place to show up in my life. As soon as I surrendered control of my life to God, everything in life started improving. As it turns out, He wrote the entire game by Himself, so He actually knows where all the cool stuff is! He knows where all the Easter eggs are at!

"So from that point, what I've done to continue to improve my life experience is examine my life for all areas in which I have not surrendered my life to God and surrender those areas. I look for all of the 'exceptions' I have written down in my life code. As soon as I do that, He wanders in, and those areas improve.

"As it turns out, God loves me and wants me to thoroughly enjoy this life experience. In order to make it enjoyable, I have to let Him have the control. To improve my life experience now is just a matter of examining all areas of it and surrendering control of it to God. Once I surrender, even the gameplay itself is different and a lot more fun."

Franco: "How so?"

Me: "Instead of life being about winning for myself, I make it about helping others win their game. This is a multiplayer game. So what God has me doing is running around the map, helping other people over the difficulties in their gameplay."

Franco: "You tell other people how to play their game?"

Me: "Oh heck no. People don't like to be told how to play their game, and they often resent me rushing over to tell them what I think they should do. No one likes that. If someone's style of gameplay is working out for them, I just leave them to their business.

"What I do is just wander around, and if someone happens to want something that I have, I just tell them how I got it. Like, they might approach me and ask, 'Hey, those are way cool level-two Elven boots of fleeting! Where'd you get those?' And I'll tell them, 'I found them in that hole in a tree over there. Hey, there are some cookies in there too!'

Franco: "Back to 'We are all beggars, showing other beggars where to find bread.'"

Me: "And cookies! There are some really good cookies out there on the map, but you have to know where to look for them. But yes, that is the style of gameplay I am involved in now. It's fun!"

Franco: "Rock on!"

The Warrior Meditation®

It is in my daily meditation practice that I improve my conscious connection with God.

Spoiler alert: if you were going to mail God a letter, His address is "right here, right now."

That is my goal in meditation practice. I am striving to be in a conscious connection with my God. The meeting location is "right here, right now," where we meet with God. It's as if I reside within a prison of my human experience, confined inside a meat puppet, trapped inside the illusion of time and space. God is already inside the visitation cubicle on the other side of the glass with His hand on the phone. My job is to get to the cubicle and pick up the phone on my side of the glass.

The difficulty of getting there is entirely on my end. God takes care of His end. I am always the one who has trouble getting there. So I have to practice daily, sometimes multiple times a day, so that I can stay in constant communion.

What I most often practice is Warrior Meditation®.

One of the first things I was told after my experience at Save A Warrior was that I needed to create a morning routine of daily practice that includes meditation. But that was only if I wanted my life to work. I obviously wanted my life to work, trusting the people who gave me this information, so I put it into practice.

I usually wake up every morning at the same time. That is me taking control of my day from the beginning of it and setting its course. There are a series of things I do. I make the bed. I read some devotionals as I sip my coffee. And then I hit a button on my phone and drop into Warrior Meditation® before I engage with anyone else.

The button I hit on my phone is the Insight Meditation Timer. https://insighttimer.com/

It's free and a huge blessing to anyone who downloads it. There are guided meditations available on it. The paid version is terrific, but the free version will allow one to configure a timer.

The Warrior Meditation® is twenty minutes long and in three phases:

Nullification
Breath Awareness
Metacognition

For the first six minutes and forty seconds, I'm going to tap my fingertips to my thumbs in ascending/descending order. It doesn't matter which direction I go, and/or if when I get to the pinky, I start over at the pointer finger or go back up with the ring finger next, as long as I'm tapping my fingertips to my thumbs.

As I tap my fingertips, I'm going to make my internal voice (the amygdala) say "Ah," and then "Vah" on the next finger tap.

The reason "Ah-Vah" was chosen as the mantra is that, theoretically, there aren't a whole lot of words in the English language that start with either of those syllables. The reciting of that mantra should not stimulate my amygdala to go wandering off on its own conversation.

Oh, but it will.

I can't sit here for six minutes and forty seconds reciting, "Ah-vah, ah-vah, ah-vah" in my head. Pretty soon, my brain starts saying, "Aren't you going to work today? At least put on pants, for God's sake."

I catch myself following those thoughts, and when I do catch myself following them, get right back to the mantra.

The first intermission chime goes off at 6:40, and the "Breath Awareness" phase begins. I quit finger-tapping and started focusing on my breath instead. With my eyes still closed, I focus on my breath coming in (through my nostrils), noticing the air filling my lungs/abdomen, pausing, and then exhaling (through the mouth). As I breathe in, I'm going to make my amygdala say, "Ah," pause and hold my breath for a moment, and as I exhale, internally say, "Vah."

I'm going to do this for another six minutes and forty seconds.

At 13:20, the next chime goes off. This is the "Metacognition" phase. I am going to simply stop reciting the "Ah-Vah" mantra. I will still focus on my breath, slowly breathing in and out, and I want to simply observe the thoughts as they pass through my mind.

At twenty minutes, the end chime goes off, and I go about with my day.

Now, my tips and tricks:

I like to use a set of Bluetooth noise-canceling headphones and often have the sound of a stream running in the background. As I'm meditating, I envision a stream flowing. There are occasional leaves floating in the stream. If I catch myself thinking about my boss, for instance, in my meditation, I will grab my boss by his throat, pick him up, put him on a leaf, and watch him float down that stream.

If I catch myself persistently thinking about someone, maybe the stream drains into a meat grinder or something. Or people use balloons. I've heard of that one. Balloons are nice, probably nicer, and more peaceful than a meat grinder, sure...

The balloon of thought rises, and they simply pop the balloon.

Eckart Tolle mentions in his powerful book (that I highly

recommend) *The Power of Now* that he pretends his mind is a mouse hole, his thoughts are mice, and he is a cat guarding the hole. He watches the hole for the next thought to pop out. No thoughts seem to pop out of the hole while he is there guarding the hole.

During the metacognition phase is when my mind is most at peace. I am as close to the phone on my side of the glass as I'm going to get, so that is when I pray.

I pray for myself first. My prayer is often the same prayer but is always heartfelt and meaningful.

I pray for wisdom. God gives wisdom freely to all who ask, and I want all that He offers me. I share my mind with God and surrender my part over to Him, praying that He fills it with wisdom. I pray that He gives me the thoughts in my mind that day and brings back my remembrance of Him.

I pray for faith and that I can feel His presence surrounding me like a blanket throughout my day.

I pray for discernment so that I can always see the truth out there in the physical world and inside myself.

I pray for humility. I pray that I never think of myself as being better than anyone I am speaking to, nor become addicted to my own significance in any manner.

I pray for obedience to His will. I pray that His will flow freely through me, not my own will and designs. I pray that I would either know His will, that my will and His will become enmeshed, or that His will includes my flaws of character. I pray that my flaws of character be made known to me, removed, or incorporated into His will.

I pray that He blesses my wife and me and keeps us free from harm.

And then I'll pray those same things for others, those around me, and any of my enemies, known or unknown.

Sometimes I pray that God shows me a person and a way that I can bless someone in such a manner that they cannot pay me back, and then I go out looking for that person.

When I do that, my day is always beautiful because I treat each person as if they are the person God has shown me to bless in such a manner.

And whatever I give to the universe always returns to me tenfold.

The After-Party— God Is Love

Me: "I always like a good after-party. That's almost its own little secret community that I've discovered. There are people who go to meetings, and then there are the people who stay after the meeting. The after-party is way more fun."

Franco: "Why is that?"

Me: "I don't know why exactly. I find the ones who linger around after the regular meeting has concluded seem to be the ones I can get really weird with for some reason. Maybe it's because I am more relaxed. As if all the people were only at the meeting because they felt like they had to attend or were very new to recovery have left, and what remains are the ones who are genuinely there because they want to be there. I can let my hair down and talk about whatever I want to talk about with no fear of judgment."

Franco: "I think you must have let all of your hair down very low at one point. You're bald."

Me: "Thank you, Franco. You are a cactus without any needles, so looks like you're bald too."

Franco: "That's probably why we get along so well. So what do you talk about in the after-party that you can't talk about in the meeting?"

Me: "Well, it's not so much that I can't talk about what I want to in a meeting. I can talk about whatever I want to. It's just not appropriate at the moment when the meeting is happening. When the meeting is over, now we can talk about whatever."

Franco: "Such as?"

Me: "Well, sometimes we share our views of God. Everyone has their own personal views on God. I have found that if I listen to the views of others, instead of judging them as wrong, my own views of God expand.

There are many theories and ideas about who God is. There is much speculation about the matter. Some are entirely certain that the only real God must be the exact one as defined by their standards and definitions. All others are wrong! People fight and die in religious wars. Lots!

There is a story in the Bible about Jesus ending a quarrel over religious regulations simply by writing something in the sand. The angry people looked at it and silently walked away. It never says what Jesus wrote; it was just something that completely silenced everyone. That was some top-level, black belt kung fu-style wisdom, whatever it was. So I often speculate."

Franco: "I have an idea."

Me: "Oh, you have an idea of what Jesus wrote? Do share."

Franco: "Are you sure?"

Me: "Stop your approval-seeking and spill your sap! No one knows what Jesus wrote, so no matter what you say, it exists in the realm of 'possibilities' that you are correct, so go ahead."

Franco: "Okay, well, remember how you said what's important to a person changes as they grow older? When you were young, it was all about survival. When you went to school, it changed popularity. That's what was important?"

Me: "I never believed I would be successfully 'popular' in school, but I thought, 'If I could just fit in, somehow...' I recall, keep going."

Franco: "As an adult, it's about accumulating stuff."

Me: "Yes, and also addiction to my own significance and status."

Franco: " Well, whatever Jesus wrote in the sand was a question that changed that all, and it made everyone silently walk away, speculating. That means what they were doing was looking inward to examine themselves for the answer to whatever Jesus wrote.

"What if Jesus wrote: 'God is none of that which you are arguing about. God is love, and that's it. I am. What God wants to know when you return to Him is, did you bring more love or more pain into this life experience for others?'

"'That's the scale. Bicker about your religious preferences later. God is love. All He wants to know is, in this game of life, did you bring more love to others or more pain? Did you make their way in life easier or more difficult? That's the scale He measures everything by. Oh, and He also says, "Talk to you all later. Please have your answer to that question when you arrive."'

"'He likes to compare your answers to all the reviews from other living things that shared this life experience with you. It's a party game He calls "judge a tree by its fruit" and a whole lot of fun, you'll see. Welp, you can all get back to your religious wars, bickering on who's right, and fighting now. Have a nice day, and see you all real soon!'

"—God"

Franco: "Well, don't just sit there. What do you think?"

Me: (Silently walks away)

Questions—Special Concerns

In other writings that I've had friends proofread for me, some of their comments were that I did not clarify the mission of Save A Warrior or go into much detail as to what that program is.

If anyone has questions about Save A Warrior, I encourage them to go to: SaveAWarrior.org

Most questions about the program will be answered on that website. If you are a veteran or first responder and have questions about attending the program, I encourage you to submit an application. After submitting an application, a window will pop up, allowing the individual to schedule a one-hour rostering call with a member of the rostering team in which all of your questions will be answered.

This is a Complex-PTS, suicidal ideation detox program that assists veterans and first responders struggling with suicidal depression, anxiety, and hypervigilance. One has to come to us with the "desperation of a drowning man," so if you're not struggling with any of those issues, this is not a "wellness retreat."

On occasion, I have applicants from individuals who have not suffered childhood trauma or severely struggling with Complex PTS and are just looking for something to "brighten up their lives a little."

I encourage those individuals to go to church, learn to meditate, or check out the following: Landmarkworldwide.com Tonyrobbins.com or one of a hundred other organizations that focus on personal development and growth.

One of my favorite personal development programs is completely free. It's called Al-Anon, and they are having those "seminars" for free all over the place. A lot of great wisdom that leads to a prosperous life can be found in those rooms.

As far as questions about any of the spiritual practices or scientific concerns raised in this book, note that at the beginning of this book, I mentioned that nothing in this text should be considered the ultimate truth, nor was I professing it to be so.

If upon reading you still wish to debate any of the material, I encourage you to address all of your concerns to larry@aintgonnarespondtothisemail.com, and I will ignore the messages in the order that they arrive.

Be blessed, and thank you for reading!
—Larry (and Franco)

SAVE A WARRIOR

saveawarrior.org

FOR VETERANS, ACTIVE DUTY MILITARY, AND OHIO FIRST RESPONDERS.

ABOUT

OUR PURPOSE

To enroll others in the possibility of completing their transformational journey.

OUR PROGRAM

More than an intervention; rather, a journey of self-discovery and transformation.

OUR TEAM

Our exceptional team combines a century of expertise, skillfully guiding recovery, integration, and transformative journeys.

Pioneered by experienced warriors, SAW is an evidence-based intervention for active duty military, returning veterans, and first responders who feel desperately alone. A holistic approach integrating proven methods and a supportive community to address the challenges related to Complex Post-Traumatic Stress. SAW represents a heroic invitation for healing that has resonated with you throughout your life.

Give us 72 hours and you will change the way you see — and live — your life.

#JustSaveOne
#WeCameBackForYou

APPLY

SAVE A WARRIOR IS A REGISTERED 501(c)-3 NONPROFIT
FEDERAL TAX ID: 45-5571507

DONATE

A Reading List

As I was digging my way out of Complex-PTS insanity, I became an avid reader. Knowledge is power. The more I understood how my brain worked, how it was all wired together, and understood how my thought patterns interacted with that brain, the easier it became to manage my life accordingly.

There is nothing new under the sun, and with trillions of people who have been through the life experience before us, we can surmise that anything anyone is currently struggling with has already been documented and written down somewhere else.

These struggles and the solution to these struggles are typically written down in things called books. This thing that you are holding now is called a book. If this is the first one you've ever picked up...

Franco: "I must say you've made a fine choice, my friend!"

Mark Twain is quoted as saying: "The man who does not read has no advantage in life over the man who cannot read." Ouch! That's right. If one knows how to read but never does, that person can expect to enjoy the lifestyle of an illiterate person.

If, on the other hand, you are struggling with Complex PTS and wish to continue on the path of healing, seeking wisdom to heal and enjoy life, the following books have blessed my life tremendously.

The Road Less Traveled by M Scott Peck
The Power of Now by Eckart Tolle
Awareness by Anthony De Mello
The Spirituality of Imperfection by Earnest Kurtz and Katherine Ketcham
Your Erroneous Zones by Wayne Dyer
The Untethered Soul by Michael Singer
Dopamine Nation by Anna Lembke
The Book of Joy by Dalai Lama and Desmond Tutu
The Physics of God by Joseph Selbie
10% Happier by Dan Harris
Complex PTSD: From Surviving to Thriving by Pete Walker
What It Is Like to Go to War by Karl Marlantes
Speaking Being by Bruce Hyde and Drew Kopp
Think Like a Monk by Jay Shetty
Way of the Peaceful Warrior by Dan Millman
Thinking Fast and Slow by Daniel Kahneman
The Shame Factor by Stephan Poulter
The Subtle Art of Not Giving a F*ck by Mark Manson
The Seat of the Soul by Gary Zukav
How to Win Friends & Influence People by Dale Carnegie
The Alchemist by Paulo Coelho

How to Be an Adult by David Richo
The Monk Who Sold His Ferrari by Robin Sharma
Change Your Thoughts, Change Your Life by Wayne Dyer
A Course in Miracles Made Easy by Alan Cohen
The Five Things We Cannot Change by David Richo
A Return to Love by Marianna Williamson
A New Earth by Eckhart Tolle
The Second Mountain by David Brooks
The Four Agreements by Miguel Ruiz
The Drama of the Gifted Child by Alice Miller
How God Changes Your Brain by Andrew Newberg
Moonwalking with Einstein by Joshua Foer
The Three Laws of Performance by Steve Zaffron and Dave Logan
Change or Die by Alan Deutschman
The Power of Vulnerability by Brene Brown
The Disappearance of the Universe by Gary Renard
The Body Keeps the Score by Bessel A Van Der Kolk
Man's Search for Meaning by Viktor Frankl
The Hero with a Thousand Faces by Joseph Campbell
7 Habits of Highly Effective People by Stephen Covey
Into the Magic Shop by James Doty
Boundaries by Henry Cloud and John Townsend
Tribe by Sebastian Junger
Shame & Guilt by Earnest Kurtz

There are a lot more, but that should get you started. Throw in *The Laundry Lists Workbook* and some other 12-step books, and you now have your summer reading list.

About the Author

Born into poverty and raised in fear on a factory farm in California, as he neared adolescence, Franco was shipped to a large chain department store in Southern Ohio, along the Ohio River on the border of Kentucky. Being slight of stature, Franco was neglected and abandoned to a back shelf of a rack in the store's Garden Center. His future seemed bleak and full of despair. Loneliness and isolation were his constant companions. As luck would have it, one day, he was spotted by a sweet, loving couple who were at the store specifically to buy Magnum XL condoms. The couple took pity on poor Franco and adopted him. They took him home and nourished him back to health. These days, Franco enjoys relaxing in his office of medium light, listening to smooth jazz, reading, and gazing out the window at the dirty, filthy weeds that grow alongside the septic tank lid.

Editor's Note:

Franco voiced displeasure and took issue upon reading this narration portraying the details of his daily life. He wished to relate that he does NOT sit around and stare out the window at weeds all day. In fact, he asked us to include his words, and I quote, "I do not just sit around and stare out the window at the dirty weeds all day! They are so vile and disgusting, filthy with their spores and perfumes, and they look so slippery. See the way their oils coat their leaves as they dance around and sashay in the breeze? I have critically important things to accomplish with my time, not just staring out at weeds. I bet, if that weed were near me, she'd probably just wrap around me like a..."

Editor: Anyway, Franco insists that he doesn't do any of that.

Chapter 1 of Book Two: "Living in Denial."